OBSERVER

Sayings
of the
EIGHTIES

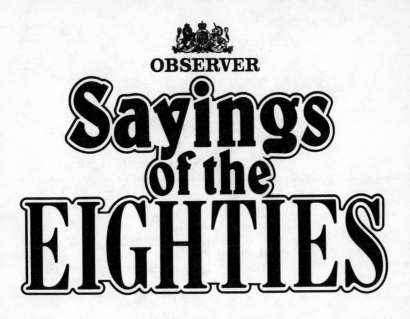

OBSERVER
Sayings
of the
EIGHTIES

Selected by Jeffrey Care

With an introduction by Hugh Cudlipp

Illustrated by Chic Jacob

W H ALLEN

Printed and bound in Great Britain by
Mackays of Chatham PLC, Chatham, Kent
for the Publishers, WH Allen & Co. Plc
Sekforde House, 175–179 St John Street, London EC1V 4LL

ISBN 1 85227 146 9

CONTENTS

INTRODUCTION

By Hugh Cudlipp

Her eye-lashes fluttered like two copulating butterflies . . . Delightful, but who first said it and about whose eye-lashes?

The irony is that when someone says something piquant, apposite or original, like Ms Mandy Rice-Davies in the witness box, it is regurgitated by the cliché-mongers until all spontaneity is drained, all sparkle dimmed.

'Well, he would, wouldn't he?' had the court and nation chuckling when the visibly demure but wise and worldly Mandy first cooed the words with a smile; they became the stock riposte of trade union and bureaucratic mediocrities stuck for an answer on Radio 4. Harold Wilson's 'A week is a long time in politics' lingers on from the beaks of political parrots. Winston Churchill's 'Never in the field of human conflict was so much owed by so many to so few' is still going the rounds; transposed, or desecrated to suit the occasion, or parodied at the opening of church fetes.

'Sayings of the Week' has been published in *The Observer* since 1917 and the criteria for selection were defined by Valerie Ferguson in the first book-of-the-best in 1978. The Sayings may be wise or witty, pompous, portentous or just plain dotty. Who said it is as significant as what was said. 'Church bells drive me mad, I can't stand them' would not have achieved the accolade of 'Sayings of the Week' had it been an off-the-cuff remark from Joan Collins or Edwina Currie. The words are Mrs Rosalind Runcie's, the wife of the Archbishop of Canterbury.

> *The bells of Hell go ting-a-ling-a-ling*
> *For you but not for me.*

The final criterion is that each Saying should have a distinct flavour of the time.

Socially, the flavour of this selection is the 80s, the going-over-the-top decade of frayed, patched and bleached Levis jeans; plastic money, instant credit, instant debt; microwave cooking, cordless phones, mass video viewing, genetic engineering and environmentalmania; topless bathing and topless TV, simulated sex after ten, in the raw after eleven; the debut of the live-in lover and the sin-in-law; drugs, mugging, terrorism and the remorseless *Grand Guignol* in Northern Ireland; public revulsion at the morals of the tabloid newspapers, and paradoxically a profitable increase in the sales of the most obnoxious of them; outrageous libels and swingeing damages; the commercial exploitation of violence and the apotheosis of the four-letter word. It became apparent that if the media in the 90s continued to trivialize the Royals as they did in the 80s the only members of the Family eventually held in public esteem would be the corgis.

Biographers will find here a more fruitful source of cosy material about the Royals than their official speeches and a more truthful source than the 'Royal watchers' of the Press. We have Prince Charles admitting in 1980 that actually sitting down and thinking is a sweat; feeling positively and frankly amazed in '81 that 'Di' was prepared to take him on; feeling all the time in '82 that he must justify his existence, and wanting to know in '85 what is actually wrong, for God's sake, with an élite.

The Duchess of York's single and singularly robust entry is less philosophical than the future monarch's. 'A woman', said Her Grace in '86, 'should have a trim waist, a good up top and enough down the bottom, but not too big.' Even the Princess Royal's 'naff off' did not beat that for mass communication.

The dewy innocence of the Princess of Wales, who is described by a Madrid genealogist elsewhere in this book as a direct descendant of Genghis Khan, is matched by the magnanimity of the mature Queen. The Princess, formerly Lady Diana Spencer, daughter of the 'eighth Earl of', considers it 'very tragic that elderly people cannot afford high electric and fuel bills'; Her Majesty's observation in '82 on Ms Koo Stark, 'she seems a very nice girl,' might have been expanded in '88 to 'and a very wealthy one, too'.

Internationally, the 80s saw the eclipse of the Cold War and the dawn of the new era in relationships. The Chief Commissar of the 'evil empire' (*pace* Reagan and Thatcher, in that order) became everybody's favourite Uncle Mikhail, a man one can 'do business with' (*pace* Thatcher and Reagan, in that order). Historians will be consulting this slim volume. I hope they find space in their tomes for President Ronnie's big-hearted remark about Comrade Gorbachov: 'I don't resent his popularity or anything else. Good Lord, I co-starred with Errol Flynn once.'

No, I have not forgotten: perish the thought. The 80s were also the decade, or the first decade, of Thatcherism, still going strong or wrong according to which of the heavies you favour on Sundays. Thatcherism has a section of its own in this anthology. Those valiant souls who fought with her or agin' her on Saint Crispin's day in 1979 will ne'er forget the years that flowed from victory; the resurrection of national pride and international influence, bizarrely accompanied by what her detractors denounce as the equivalent of a cost-effective valuation of white sticks for the blind and of biscuits for their guide dogs; a move from the monopoly of nationalization to the monopolies of privatization; the demise of Luddite trade unionism; value-for-money over need-for-money; the improvement in the standard of living for the better off; the swift rise of the upwardly mobile and their swifter fall; the elevation of Young of Graffham to the House of Lords as 'one of us' and the levitation (usually attributed to supernatural intervention) of the Tory wets to the same place because they were 'one of them'.

Mrs T on Mrs T is a joy to savour, a daisy chain of illuminating asides which chivalry obliges me to acclaim as confidence in a woman but curmudgeonly critics would deride as megalomania in a man. 'The thing I notice is that I tend to look at things much more logically than my colleagues ('80) . . . Our policies are perfectly right. There will be no change ('80) . . . I'll stay until I'm tired of it. So long as Britain needs me I shall never be tired of it ('82) . . . I am extraordinarily patient, provided I get my own way in the end ('82) . . . I do not think I could take more than another ten years of such years as this ('82) . . . I think, historically, the term "Thatcherism" will be seen as a compliment ('85) . . . In another five years I will have been in 11½ years, then someone else will carry the torch ('85) . . . Let me say this – If you want someone weak you don't want me.' ('86)

My favourite Mrs T-ism: 'I think I have become a bit of an institution – you know, the sort of thing people expect to be around the place.' Connoisseurs of the PM's more endearing conceits will be happy to know that 'Sayings of the 80s' has conserved for posterity the domestic pavement leak outside No 10 Downing Street by 'Er Inside in '89. The regal plurality of her announcement of her parental promotion, 'We have become a grandmother,' is thus assured the immortality enjoyed by her Majesty Queen Victoria's 'We are not amused.'

The Editor of *The Observer* may confidently reserve a section on Thatcherism in 'Sayings of the 90s', though covering a shorter period than the present book.

I knew Gary Hart was in trouble when he changed his campaign slogan from 'Let the People decide' to 'Who's asking you?'

> *Ronald Reagan*   3.4.88

Of the four wars in my lifetime, none came about because the US was too strong.

> *Ronald Reagan*   29.6.80

I'm off to Elba to await the call from the mainland.

> *Bruce Babbitt, withdrawing from the US presidential primaries*
> 21.2.88

A campaign rally in California is three people around a television set.

> *Robert Shrum, US speech writer.*   2.11.86

His foreparents came to America in immigrant ships. My foreparents came to America in slave ships. But whatever the original ships, we are both in the same boat tonight.

> *Jesse Jackson*   24.7.88

New York's like a disco, but without the music.

> *Miss Elaine Stritch*   17.2.80

American taxpayers make it possible for a Soviet housewife to buy American produced food at a price lower than any American housewife.

> *George Schultz, on US grain sales to Russia.* 10.8.86

America isn't finished: her best days have just begun.

> *Ronald Reagan* 1.2.87

Washington could not tell a lie; Nixon could not tell the truth; Reagan cannot tell the difference.

> *Mort Sahl* 18.10.87

It bewilders Americans to be hated.

> *Mr Lance Morrow* 13.1.80

Every time I get near government it strikes me that it just doesn't work.

> *Joseph P. Kennedy III, US Congressional candidate.* 25.5.86

That's the nice thing about this job. You get to quote yourself shamelessly. If you don't, Larry Speakes will.

> *Ronald Reagan* 17.4.88

We're an ideal political family, as accessible as Disneyland.

> *Maureen Reagan* 26.8.84

Ronnie is a very soft touch, and I don't want anyone taking advantage of him.

> *Nancy Reagan* 25.11.84

The United States is the best and fairest and most decent nation on the face of the earth.

> *George Bush* 8.5.88

Great things happen in small places. Jesus was born in Bethlehem. Jesse Jackson was born in Greenville.

> *Jesse Jackson* 13.3.88

There are a whole group of people in Europe who are constantly anti-American, who have never forgiven us for the Marshall Plan.

> *General Vernon Walters*   20.4.86.

There's a lot to be said for being *nouveau riche* and the Reagans mean to say it all.

> *Gore Vidal*   26.4.81

I don't resent his popularity or anything else. Good Lord, I co-starred with Errol Flynn once.

> *President Reagan, on Mikhail Gorbachov*   6.12.87

Most Americans believe they are the only good people in the world and everyone should be like them. Americans are standing tall, whatever that means. It's childish.

> *former Senator William Fulbright*   30.11.86

The bear is a thing we can't control, one of the only things that Americans are afraid of.

> *Chris Servheen, US Grizzly Bear Recovery Program*   10.1.84

We've got the kind of President who thinks arms control means some kind of deodorant.

> *Congresswoman Patricia Schroeder*   9.8.87

There is nothing wrong with America that together we can't fix.

> *President Reagan*   22.2.81

My basic rule is that I want people who don't want a job in government.

> *President-elect Reagan*   16.11.80

The greatest vacuum in American politics is to the right of Ronald Reagan.

> *Patrick Buchanan, White House Director of Communications* 8.2.87

I turn back to your ancient prophets in the Old Testament for the signs foretelling Armageddon and I find myself wondering if we're the generation that's going to see that come about.

> *President Reagan*   4.12.83

The United States presidential system just won't work any more. Anyone who gets in under it ought not to be allowed to serve.

> *Gore Vidal*   31.8.80

If you understand the silent generation, you understand Mike Dukakis.

> *Richard Gaines, biographer*   5.6.88

I'd like people to know I'm voting for Michael Dukakis.

> *Robert Redford*   28.8.88

This mad dog of the Middle East.

> *President Reagan on Colonel Qadhafi*   13.4.86

I served with Jack Kennedy. I knew Jack Kennedy. Jack Kennedy was a friend of mine. Senator, you're no Jack Kennedy.

> *Senator Lloyd Bentsen to Dan Quayle*   9.10.88

Everybody should have a Ronald Reagan in their lives.

> *Nancy Reagan*   9.2.86

I find he's not only a barbarian, but he's flaky.

> *President Reagan on Colonel Qadhafi*   12.1.86

We meant to change a nation, and instead we changed a world.

> *Ronald Reagan*   15.1.89

THE ARTS

The arts are to Britain what sunshine is to Spain.

Sir William Rees-Mogg 31.3.85

At one point I got the musical seven year itch. You know, after you play seven years, you want to conduct.

Itzhak Perlman 9.10.88

Bartok was a nice man.

Benny Goodman 29.6.80

When I was a little boy they called me a liar but now that I am a grown up they call me a writer.

Isaac Bashevis Singer 17.7.83

Film was and is still a romantic business, just as life is romantic.

Katherine Hepburn 4.10.87

Before I was shot I always thought that I was more half-there than all-there.

Andy Warhol 13.7.86

Only really very tall conductors can deal adequately with slow music.

> *Neville Marriner*   17.3.85

Art has to move you and design does not, unless it's a good design for a bus.

> *David Hockney*   30.10.88.

When you can freely quote a bad notice and it is funny, then it's an exorcism.

> *Diana Rigg*   28.2.82

If it's a good script, I'll do it. And if it's a bad script, and they pay me enough, I'll do it.

> *George Burns*   13.11.88

Free verse has come to represent democracy, equal opportunity and self-expression. But in bulk, and unaware of the forms from which it has been 'freed', it can be extremely depressing.

> *A. S. Byatt*   27.11.88

The director is the most overrated artist in the world.

> *Orson Welles*   7.3.82

The task of the artist at any time is uncompromisingly simple – to discover what has not yet been done, and to do it.

> *Craig Raine*   21.8.88

We actors are the damned of the earth.

> *Sophia Loren*   31.8.80

People think a cartoon is something that appears in a newspaper, but to me a cartoon encompasses all the great artists.

> *Ralph Steadman*   4.12.88

If New York is the Big Apple, tonight Hollywood is the Big Nipple.

> *Bernardo Bertolucci, collecting his Oscar*   17.4.88

I'm usually called jack-of-all-trades by people who are scarcely jacks of one.

Jonathan Miller   24.4.88

Critics are more malicious about poetry than about other books — maybe because so many manqué poets write reviews.

Elizabeth Jennings   27.12.87

I have always thought my pictures were too expensive.

David Hockney   30.7.80

The Parthenon without the marbles is like a smile with a tooth missing.

Neil Kinnock   10.1.84

His comedy was based on truth, which is the essence of all great comedy.

Ian Carmichael, on Peter Sellers   30.7.80

I know how foolish critics can be, being one myself.

Anthony Burgess   2.11.80

There just isn't enough interesting work for women in the theatre.

Miss Glenda Jackson.   17.2.80

Space or science fiction has become a dialect for our time.

Doris Lessing   13.11.88

One of the joys of going to the movies was that it was trashy and we should never lose that.

Oliver Stone   21.2.88.

When I started as a writer there was a feeling that money was something you would start to worry about when you were 45.

Tom Wolfe   14.2.88

I see Shaw as a man who was dealt quite a faulty hand, but played it brilliantly.

Michael Holroyd, biographer   4.10.87

Comedy needs kindness.

John Sessions 23.8.87

Some of the best Russian writing is twentieth-century poetry and not many people are aware of that.

Joseph Brodsky, Nobel Prizewinner 25.10.87

The whole business of comedy is exciting just because it is dangerous, because you are walking on a knife edge.

Geraldine McEwan 10.4.88

I have the greatest admiration for British musicians but it is time they complained.

Sir George Solti 15.6.80

It happens to everybody, that point when you can't play the guy who comes in carrying a gun and cleans up the bar any more.

Anthony Quinn 20.11.83

All English actors know that the ultimate challenge is a classical text.

Simon Callow 10.7.88

I haven't had a hit film since Joan Collins was a virgin.

Burt Reynolds 27.3.88

I don't mean much to the Rambo crowd.

Woody Allen 14.8.88

The two glories of this country are the English landscape and English literature.

Kenneth Baker 13.4.86

You can only write about what bites you.

Tom Stoppard 15.1.84

I stopped going to see my films when I began to watch what was bad about my face, my neck, my body, my voice.

Katharine Hepburn 20.7.86.

I am totally opposed to admission charges.

> *Neil MacGregor, new Director of the National Gallery*   3.8.86

Western culture is not suitable for us without modification.

> *Mr Joshua Nkomo*   3.2.80

I think very often why people are idolising the rage in Picasso is because it legitimises their own.

> *Arianna Stassinopoulos Huffington*   10.7.88

In order to do good work, it has to worry you a lot.

> *André Previn*   7.10.84

Children love to be frightened. Fairy tales are a deadly pleasure.

> *Edna O'Brien*   21.11.82

I rather think poetry has given me up, which is a great sorrow to me, but not an enormous, crushing sorrow. It's rather like going bald.

> *Philip Larkin*   15.4.84

The age of the book is almost gone.

> *George Steiner*   3.7.88

To finish is both a relief and a release from an extraordinarily pleasant prison.

> *Dr Robert Burchfield, on completing the Oxford English Dictionary*   11.5.86

What's a cult? It just means not enough people to make a minority.

> *Robert Altman*   11.5.86

In my opinion all BBC drama is now heavily biased against the Establishment and particularly against this Government.

> *Ian Curteis, dramatist*   5.10.86

This was a role I felt I was born to play.

> *Peter O'Toole on 'Macbeth.'*   14.12.80

To be a judge you don't have to know about books, you have to be skilled at picking shrapnel out of your head.

> *Joanna Lumley on the Booker prize*   17.11.85

If I were just starting, I could not even have got into a veterinary college.

> *James Herriot*   19.6.83

The farther north you go, the better dancing you see.

> *Joe Loss*   25.5.80.

Few persons who have ever sat for a portrait can have felt anything but inferior while the process is going on.

> *Anthony Powell*   9.1.83

A writer doesn't write to help humanity, but to help himself.

> *Graham Greene*   23.8.81

Rightly or wrongly, wars make for better reading than peace does.

> *A. J. P. Taylor*   5.7.81

Two people sitting in a chair talking about the end of the world is cheaper to do than showing the end of the world.

> *Ken Russell*   12.7.81

I'm apt to forget my age. The other day I saw Kingsley Amis and asked how well he knew D. H. Lawrence. His eyes bulged and his face grew purple.

> *Peter Quennell*   25.9.88

I cringe when critics say I'm a master of the popular novel. What's an unpopular novel?

> *Irwin Shaw*   6.3.83

I think that if a third of all the novelists and maybe two-thirds of all the poets now writing dropped dead suddenly, the loss to literature would not be great.

> *Charles Osborne, departing Arts Council literary chief*   3.11.85

If Wagner is to be punished for his antisemitism, then he is being punished right now in his big centennial year at Bayreuth, where there are only Jewish conductors.

Daniel Barenboim 6.11.83

All novel-writing is to some extent day-dreaming.

Mr Francis King 20.1.80

I guess I think that films have to be made totally by fascists. There's no room for democracy in making a film.

Don Pennebaker 31.7.88

I never thought that I would earn enough money from my pictures to make a living.

Francis Bacon 26.5.85

If you call something the National Theatre it is inviting people to throw bricks at it.

Richard Eyre, director 17.8.86

It's the BBC's answer to musical chairs, except that when the music stops we add another chair, not take one away.

BBC executive on top staff appointments 31.1.82

I do not quite see how a council whose average age is 60 is going to understand what Channel 4 is about.

Michael Grade on the Broadcasting Standards Council 14.8.88

I'd be uneasy if the people I impersonated congratulated me too much.

Pamela Stephenson 7.6.81

I'm all in favour of making up words if the one you want doesn't exist.

Tom Sharpe 10.5.81

If I wasn't an actor I'd probably be a psychopath.

Terence Stamp 2.11.86

No art is worth much which does not aim to change the world.

> *Lindsay Anderson* 23.3.86

I'm very deeply depressed to hear that art students are interested in being successful.

> *Patrick Heron* 29.5.88

There is no highbrow in any lowbrow, but there is a lot of lowbrow in every highbrow.

> *Eric Sevareid (quoting Justice Frankfurter)* 22.5.88

I cannot get in and out of aircraft toilets but on three and a half hour flights I can hold out.

> *Luciano Pavarotti on his preference for Concorde* 2.7.87

I went to Hollywood once to write for Deanna Durbin. I wasn't impressed at all. Beverly Hills was just Golders Green with sunshine.

> *Vivian Ellis, composer* 9.8.87

When I was 25, Bartok needed me, a young man who would get up on the podium, play his music and be whistled at for it.

> *Antal Dorati* 13.4.86

I still write a fugue every day.

> *Anthony Burgess* 27.10.85

I feel that readiness is all. You get a sort of arrogance, a balance, to do your work as well as possible.

> *Kenneth Branagh* 11.9.88

You know, sometimes I don't even like music.

> *Sir William Walton* 28.3.82

If I had been someone not very clever, I would have done an easier job like publishing. That's the easiest job I can think of.

> *A. J. Ayer* 9.9.84

Shakespeare's plays were the most popular in his time, just as EastEnders is the most popular play for us now.

> *Peter Holland, fellow of Trinity Hall, Cambridge*   14.11.86

For the young people music and poetry can sway you more than politics.

> *Benjamin Zephaniah, poet*   18.9.88

The festival is élitist, and I'm perfectly happy that it should be.

> *George Christie, Chairman, Glyndebourne Productions*   1.6.80

A country without art may appear to be sophisticated and rich, but its wealth is only on the surface.

> *Elimo Njau, East African artist*   14.12.80

The English language is like a juggernaut truck that goes on regardless.

> *Dr Robert Burchfield, Editor-in-Chief, Oxford English dictionaries*   25.10.81

A number of mediocrities have received grants from us in the past few years and we ought not to have been handing out money to those writers.

> *Charles Osborne, literature director, Arts Council*   5.4.81

I hadn't the courage for suicide, but it became a habit with me to visit troubled places.

> *Graham Greene*   5.10.80

Beethoven is still available to be contacted.

> *John Lill*   17.8.80

Writers don't need love. All they require is money.

> *John Osborne*   5.4.81

The artist, as you know, in his heart of hearts is right-wing and reactionary.

> *Franco Zeffirelli*   14.12.86

The paragraph is a great art form. I'm very interested in paragraphs and I write paragraphs very, very carefully.

Iris Murdoch   21.9.80

If a film costs five million dollars and looks as if it cost 10 million, that's good; but if it looks as if it cost only four million, that's wrong.

Mr Clint Eastwood   21.9.80

There is scarcely any book so bad that nothing can be learnt from it.

Enoch Powell   18.8.85

Writing a poem is like a short love affair, writing a short story like a long love affair, writing a novel like a marriage.

Amos Oz   21.7.85

Everybody writes a book too many.

Mordecal Richler   9.6.85

It is a sad feature of modern life that only women for the most part have time to write novels, and they seldom have much to write about.

Auberon Waugh   21.6.81

I write when I'm inspired, and I see to it that I'm inspired at nine o'clock every morning.

Peter DeVries   28.9.80

I'm going to live forever. Geniuses don't die.

Salvador Dali   20.7.86

I still have to fight this idea that I'm just a drummer.

Ringo Starr   25.5.80

We're not talking Tolstoy here.

Maureen Dean, author of 'Washington Wives'.   27.3.88

I'm the end of the line; absurd and appalling as it may seem, serious New York theatre has died in my lifetime.

Arthur Miller   15.1.89

I feel I'm a small part of a national monument.

> *Michael Yeats on the 50th anniversary of his father's death*
> 29.1.89

Poetry has everything to do with speeches, a knowledge that words are magic, that words, like children, have the power to make dance the dullest beanbag of a heart.

> *Peggy Noonan, US presidential speechwriter*   22.1.89

BROADCASTING

Bad language causes more upset among viewers than violence.

Leslie Halliwell, ITV 13.9.81

I am handing something very special to you. If you mess it up I will personally come round and throttle you.

Jeremy Isaacs to Michael Grade regarding Channel 4. 22.11.87

I consider television to be a bigger threat than hooliganism to the future of football.

Brian Clough 11.8.85

If they do televise it they will only televise a House which would be quite different from the House of Commons we know.

Margaret Thatcher 14.2.88

We think a quid a week for the TV service would be a very fair sum to charge.

Alasdair Milne, Managing Director, BBC-TV 31.8.80

We are told there is absolutely no proof that violence on TV has any effect on people's behaviour. That, as we all know, is palpable nonsense.

The Prince of Wales 18.9.88

Dan Archer is the fabric of the nation, but we might still kill him off.

> *BBC spokesman* 15.8.82

Quite frankly I think people want to watch sex and some form of violence on television. If they've come home after a boring day at work, they don't want to watch a gardening programme.

> *Christopher Ellison, actor* 13.11.88

'EastEnders' is really a contemporary morality series.

> *Alasdair Milne* 8.12.85

The fault of the BBC is not treachery but smugness.

> *Jo Grimond* 23.5.82

Impartiality in broadcast journalism is a withering plant in need of some sustaining care and attention.

> *John Birt* 10.4.88

I never thought I would be in tears over 'Crossroads', but I am.

> *Patti Caldwell* 3.4.88

I saved TV-am and now I am here to save the BBC

> *Roland Rat* 6.10.85

TV has something in common with the world of racing: it is crowded with untrustworthy characters, and bristles with opportunities to cheat.

> *Paul Johnson* 4.7.81

It has always struck me as rather strange that in a supposedly Christian country an agnostic was considered preferable to a Roman Catholic for the top job in the BBC.

> *Sir Hugh Greene* 9.5.82

When they ring you up at the BBC and ask you out to lunch then you know you've been fired.

> *Jack de Manio* 1.2.81

Nothing can really change until the class system does.

Shirley Williams 12.4.81

It has always been far too expensive to improve the educational standards of working class children significantly.

Sir Angus Maude 19.4.81

The worst fault of the working classes is telling their children they're not going to succeed, saying: 'There is a life, but it's not for you.'

John Mortimer 22.5.88

I don't pretend that I was born in Surbiton and my father was a Justice of the Peace.

Michael Caine 22.9.85

The cry of equality pulls everyone down.

Iris Murdoch 13.9.87

My mother came from Nashville, Tennessee, and try as she would she couldn't obliterate her accent. Just like Margaret. Just like Ted.

Lord Hailsham 18.10.81

No one can change their origin. If they do they become foreigners for the rest of their lives.

Erno Rubrik 30.8.87

'You're not a working-class lad. You're a good writer.'

Shirley Williams to Roy Hattersley. 8.12.85

Best-selling poet dies in private hospital.

The Morning Star on the death of Philip Larkin 8.12.85

In my time there have been four Tory and two Labour masters of foxhounds in Parliament.

Jo Grimond 15.8.82

What I want to know is; what is actually wrong with an élite, for God's sake?

Prince Charles 17.11.85

I think it is probably still true that nationalism is stronger than any class feeling.

Fenner Brockway 26.7.81

The working classes are never embarrassed by money – only the absence of it.

Ken Livingstone 13.9.87

The lower middle class was a class waiting room, nobody knew how to behave or what attitudes to have in the still waters of mediocrity.

John Boorman 30.8.87.

The thing I value about Wales and the Welsh background is that it has always been a genuinely more classless society than many people present England as being.

Sir Geoffrey Howe 4.11.86

I don't see any harm in being middle class, I've been middle class all my life and have benefited from it.

Lord Hailsham 20.3.83

CRIME & POLICE

I am an honest and truthful man who puts his trust in God and fears nothing from any complaint.

James Anderton, Chief Constable of Manchester 22.12.85

Juries are not skilled in distinguishing between good and bad policemen.

Lord Devlin 30.7.80

No one stays apolitical for very long once they have experienced a charge by French riot police.

A university lecturer in Paris 14.12.86

Not everybody votes according to their own pocket.

Ian Wrigglesworth, MP 24.8.88

We are losing control of the streets. It sometimes takes 10 men in a van to deal with a problem which the absence of one man has produced.

Roger Birch, Sussex Chief Constable 9.10.88

People have got to calm down and just think of this person as another human being.

Lord Longford on Myra Hindley 23.11.86

I would like to see a return to the good old fashioned policeman: 16 stone and six feet four inches tall.

> *James Horsfall, governor of Oxford prison*   26.6.83

The police were to blame for what happened on Sunday night and what they got was a bloody good hiding.

> *Haringey Council leader Bernie Grant on the Tottenham riot* 13.10.85

If Jesus were here today He may well have spoken in terms similar to the ones I used.

> *James Anderton*   25.1.87

Most dangerous criminals are like elephants, difficult to define but easy to recognise.

> *Lord Justice Lawton*   30.8.81

If a woman is attacked, her best weapon is her lungs.

> *Chief Inspector Keith Killbride, West Yorkshire Crime Prevention Bureau*   24.2.80

The police are the only 24-hour social service in the country.

> *Commander Alex Marnoch, new police chief at Brixton* 20.2.83

I cannot pretend that I have not heard Heathrow described as 'Thievesrow.'

> *Judge Brian Gibbens, QC.*   17.2.80

I'm still available.

> *Harry Allen, official hangman*   26.6.83

Truncheons are flimsy things.

> *Inspector Douglas Hopkins, Special Patrol Group*   11.5.80

If I had shot him it would have been in anger and I'm not trained that way.

> *PC Trevor Lock*   18.1.81

The trigger of today's outburst of crime and violence . . . lies in the era and attitudes of post-war funk which gave birth to the 'permissive society.'

> Norman Tebbit   17.11.85

As a means of reducing the level of crime, will you consider the re-invention of a modern system of stocks?

> Tony Marlow to the Home Secretary   24.4.88

Even the most hardened criminal a few years ago would help an old lady across the road and give her a few quid if she was skint.

> Charles Kray   9.2.86

There is a lot wrong with society today. It's depraved.

> Peter Sutcliffe   24.5.81

I think we policemen are far too ready to assume a suspect's guilt in the early stages when we should be assuming his innocence.

> Sir Peter Imbert   17.7.88

It would make much more sense at demonstrations if the police carried banners saying 'Remember Blair Peach,' rather than the Lefties.

> Mr Auberon Waugh   4.5.80

If you mention community relations to the ordinary policeman, he either falls about laughing or starts cursing.

> Rev Robert Nind, Vicar of Brixton   19.4.81

If the circumstances are justified, you can get your blow in first to prevent attack.

> Mr Justice Croom-Johnson, summing up in the Stephen Waldorf case   20.11.85

A little bit of judicial violence would reduce public violence by a massive amount.

> Mr Tony Marlow, MP.   21.3.82

I once thought it might be nice to be a detective at New Scotland Yard, but I also wanted to go on the stage.

Peter Imbert   21.2.88

Political activists are a destabilising influence and a threat to public order.

Sir Kenneth Newman, Metropolitan Police Commissioner
3.7.83

I was brought up to hold doors open for ladies.

John Gotti, alleged Mafia chief   19.1.86

One gets the impression from the popular Press that rape has become the British national pastime.

Lord Wigoder   24.1.82

Forget about the cosy image of Dixon of Dock Green.

Jim Jardine, Police Federation   19.7.81

We rarely have a murder on the Metro. It's never been more than three or four a year.

Nadine Joly, security chief, Paris Metro   10.1.82

Being in prison is a singularly relaxing situation.

Lord Kagan   17.8.80

Our aim is to ensure that there can be no hiding place for criminals anywhere in the world.

Douglas Hurd on extradition   20.7.86

DEFENCE

Detente is like the race in 'Alice in Wonderland' where everyone had to have a prize.

>   *Lord Carrington*   9.3.80

Even an inaccurate missile is quite a deterrent.

>   *US Defence Secretary Caspar Weinberger*   11.10.81

Deterrence may be accepted as the lesser of two evils, without in any way regarding it as good in itself.

>   *Cardinal Hume*   6.11.83

I believe one has to trust those in charge of the security services.

>   *Margaret Thatcher*   30.11.86

If it is necessary to defend the freedom and security of Western Europe and this country then I would use atomic weapons.

>   *President Carter*   21.9.80

The navy isn't all wind and spray and yo-heave-ho.

>   *Admiral Sir John Treacher, on his appointment as Chairman of the Playboy Club*   12.7.81

I am convinced that the Force is with us.

> *General James Abrahamson, US Star Wars Chief* 23.2.86

Arms control so easily becomes an incantation rather than policy.

> *Richard Perle after his resignation as US assistant secretary of defence* 15.3.87

The history of humanity, I think, cannot be allowed to end in an atomic inferno.

> *Klaus Fuchs* 24.8.88

To adopt the unilateral disarmament option would be akin to behaving like a virgin in a brothel.

> *Mr David Penhaligan MP (Lib)* 14.9.80

Preparing for suicide is not a very intelligent means of defence.

> *Monsignor Bruce Kent* 10.8.86

There would almost certainly be major wars going on in Europe over the past few decades if we hadn't got nuclear weapons.

> *Rev Richard Harries, Bishop-elect of Oxford* 11.1.87

You cannot create nuclear-free zones by putting up signs on the lampposts of Lambeth.

> *David Steel* 28.9.86

The only profession that is praised throughout the Bible is that of the soldier.

> *Letter in the Daily Telegraph* 8.8.82

It is inconceivable we should refuse United States aircraft and pilots the right to defend their own people.

> *Margaret Thatcher* 20.4.86

Belgian servicewomen are extremely upset over the affectionate terms by which they are addressed by their male colleagues, who regularly call them darling, treasure, baby or other endearing terms.

> *Belgian MP Paul Devlies* 14.6.81

NATO will never fire the first shot. If it can maintain the resolve of the past it will never have to fire the second.

> *Lord Carrington*   2.6.86

Here a new arms race is waiting to get its starting signal. But only a dreamer can believe you can arms race the Soviet Union to death.

> *Helmut Schmidt, on Star Wars*   14.9.86

I see no way in which we could deter in Europe without nuclear weapons.

> *General John Galvin, Nato Supreme Commander*   20.9.87

The important thing when you are going to do something brave is to have someone on hand to witness it.

> *Michael Howard MC, Chichele Professor of the History of War, Oxford.*   18.5.80

Like a curving ram's horn, the cold war is now growing inwards into the warriors' own brains.

> *E. P. Thompson*   20.11.83

British Forces are like permanent tourists.

> *Sir Joshua Hassan, former Chief Minister of Gibraltar*   5.2.89

Mass unemployment is wrong, morally wrong.

> *Mr Heath*   18.10.81

A hundred thousand pounds is nothing nowadays.

> *Mr George Talbot, ex-docker and amateur gambler*   16.8.81.

As a result of recent events, neither raising, nor reducing, nor leaving interest rates as they are, makes sense.

> *Samuel Brittan*   24.4.88

Plenty of things bore me but money is top of the list.

> *Kingsley Amis*   26.4.87

A bunch of promoted bank clerks who think they are Mandarins.

> *Lord Beloff on the Treasury*   22.11.87

No Chancellor until this one has come to the House and said that because he has money available to him the rich will get the benefits and the poor will make the sacrifices.

> *Gordon Brown, MP.*   1.5.88

Wealth creation is often not seen as a suitable pursuit for a nice person.

> *Sir Denis Rooke, Chairman of British Gas* 11.1.81

If freedom were not so economically efficient it certainly wouldn't stand a chance.

> *Milton Friedman* 1.3.87

Sometimes this job is just one thing after another.

> *Nigel Lawson* 4.12.88

Many people would be prepared to pay more taxes – and forgo tax cuts – in order to help divert resources to the poor.

> *Archbishop of Canterbury* 8.2.87

Money is as much a reality as the Blessed Trinity.

> *Monsignor Ralph Brown, co-ordinator* 28.6.81

If we imagine the UK can get by with a bunch of people in smocks showing tourists around medieval castles we are, quite frankly, out of our minds.

> *Sir John Harvey-Jones* 6.4.86

I would need some persuading before an industrial or commercial company is allowed to take control of a bank.

> *Robin Leigh-Pemberton* 18.10.87

If no wealth is being created, then arguments about its distribution are academic.

> *Lord Scanlon* 1.3.81

You must give the nationalised industries away.

> *Professor Milton Friedman* 2.3.80

The black economy has played a very large part in keeping this country going.

> *Lord Scarman* 7.11.86

Having money is rather like being a blonde. It is more fun but not vital.

Mary Quant   2.11.86

The Budget was brilliant, quite the most brilliant we have seen. Brilliant in conception, brilliant in drafting, brilliant in delivery.

Margaret Thatcher   31.7.88

Never before has any government been more determined to stamp out abuse, malpractice and fraud in the City.

Paul Channon   25.1.87

My first reaction is that this will prove all the suspicions that the public might have that Wall Street is just full of a bunch of insiders taking advantage of them.

John Gutfreund, Chairman of Salomon Brothers   23.11.86

I would not take too much notice of teenage scribblers in the City who jump up and down in an effort to get Press attention.

Nigel Lawson   3.7.88

EDUCATION

Of all human activities, education is the one most likely to give rise to cant, pomposity and fraudulent expertise.

John Rae, Head Master of Westminster 19.6.83

It is no exaggeration to describe plain English as a fundamental tool of government.

Margaret Thatcher 13.3.88

We have a very serious problem on our hands, with many graduates leaving university without knowing the difference between an adverb and a preposition.

Colin MacCabe, Cambridge English Faculty 25.1.81

Oxford is, and always has been, full of cliques, full of factions, and of a particular non-social snobbishness.

Mrs Mary Warnock 2.11.80

I am sick to death of education in this country being knocked, largely for political purposes.

Edward Heath 6.12.87

If history could be taught in such a fashion that it would help create harmony among people, rather than division and hatred, it would serve this and other nations better.

> *Dr Desmond Moran, Coroner, Sligo*   13.1.80

Private funding has become essential if Oxford is to remain in that small league of perhaps 10 world-class universities.

> *Lord Jenkins of Hillhead*   8.5.88

Barnsley Grammar School did for education what myxomatosis did for rabbits.

> *Michael Parkinson*   6.2.81

Girls and boys grow up more normally together than apart.

> *Daphne Rae, wife of the Head Master of Westminster*   8.5.88

In the field of philosophy the best way of getting a job is to sit in the Bodleian.

> *Dr Julius Tomin*   28.8.88

Education by beating, and especially of young people, raises special objections.

> *Cardinal Glemp*   5.6.83

You see the headlines saying kids are illiterate. They're not illiterate, they're just processing information in a different way.

> *American cable TV executive*   10.10.82

I don't see it as the duty of government for every child up to the age of five to be looked after by the government.

> *Sir Keith Joseph*   1.11.81

It's very different from living in academia in Oxford. We called someone vicious in the *Times Literary Supplement*. We didn't know what vicious was.

> *Aung San Suu Kyi, opposition leader, on returning to Burma*
> 25.9.88

Academic staff rather enjoy coming to conclusions, but they don't like coming to decisions at all.

> *Lord Annan*   6.2.81

Ninety-nine per cent of Oxford students cannot afford drugs. Most are worried where their next cup of coffee is coming from.

> *Viscount Althorp*   22.6.86

The first class at Oxford, where I have examined, is an over-rated mark.

> *Lord Dacre (Hugh Trevor-Roper)*   28.6.81

I cannot believe that any Westminster boy is gathering material for a novel about his schooldays.

> *John Rae, Head Master of Westminster School*   4.11.82

My advice to members is carry on caning.

> *David Hart, general Secretary of the National Association of Head Teachers*   28.2.82

What shall I do? My Dad will kill me.

> *Jade Jagger after being expelled from school*   29.5.88

Huge numbers of students are being influenced by the biased one-sidedness of contemporary sociology. They are being systematically de-skilled for effective work and trained to be nothing better than critical saboteurs.

> *Professor David Marsland*   19.7.87

We have absolutely no philosophy on thrashing. My partners and I were all thrashed at school.

> *Dai Llewellyn on buying the Bognor Cane Company*   19.7.87

Abolish the independent schools and you abolish some of the riches of European civilisation.

> *John Thorn, headmaster of Winchester*   27.9.81

While in other respects the United Kingdom is prospering, it seems that the pursuit of natural knowledge is to be allowed to diminish.

> *Sir George Porter*   6.12.87

We have a better record than the university, on the whole, on recruiting women and people from the North.

Andrew McCulloch, president of the Oxford Union   25.9.88

I am one of these people for whom corporal punishment actually worked.

Prince Charles   26.7.81

We have for too long underestimated the importance of craft skills.

Kenneth Baker   4.9.88

ENVIRONMENT

Whenever I drive in Southern England today the place is being torn up and torn apart.

Michael Heseltine 20.3.88

Our English countryside is one of the most heavily man-made habitats in Europe. To make it into a green museum would be to belie its whole history.

Nicholas Ridley 6.11.88

Leaving the inner cities to fester results in an ever-increasing spiral of decay, of poor physical and mental health and general low morale.

Prince Charles 2.11.86

What is proposed is a monstrous carbuncle on the face of a much loved and elegant friend.

Prince Charles, on the design for the National Gallery extension 3.7.84

Mount Everest is now littered with junk from bottom to top.

Sir Edmund Hillary 4.11.82

We do not intend to allow developers to devour our green and pleasant land.

> *Michael Jopling*   15.3.87

The Conservative Party is the natural party of conservation.

> *Kenneth Baker, Secretary of State for the Environment*   29.9.85

You have to give this much to the Luftwaffe – when it knocked down our buildings it did not replace them with anything more offensive than rubble. We did that.

> *Prince Charles*   6.12.87

To me it's more like a hi-tech version of a Victorian prison.

> *Prince Charles opening the Plessey microchip factory at Roborough*   10.5.87

When we read that over the next 60 years, if we go on as we are doing, something like a third of all the forms of life at present living on this planet may be extinct, can we feel anything but a sense of cosmic horror?

> *Prince Charles*   27.3.88

Architects seem to cry: 'When I hear the word culture I reach for my concrete mixer.'

> *Critic Rodney Gradidge on the Barbican Centre*   7.3.82

Contrary to popular mythology, it is not my Department's mission in life to tarmac over the whole of England.

> *Paul Channon*   25.9.88

Can anyone draw up a list of five buildings in London worth a detour to see, which have been put up since the war?

> *Mr Jo Grimond, MP.*   31.5.81

Had we gone the way of France and got 60 per cent of our electricity from nuclear power, we should not have environmental problems.

> *Margaret Thatcher*   30.10.88

We are sitting on a powder keg in the inner cities.

> *Bernie Grant, MP.* 12.7.87

All architects want to live beyond their death.

> *Philip Johnson* 26.7.87

Tomorrow our own children and grandchildren will find themselves condemned to live in slums unless something is done now.

> *Lord Scarman* 11.1.87

There is no transport system on this planet that breaks even, let alone makes a profit.

> *Ken Livingstone* 20.12.81

The Irish Sea is naturally radioactive, the Sellafield discharges are less radioactive than the sea they are discharged into.

> *Cecil Parkinson* 29.11.87

To copy buildings from a bygone age, for no other reason than familiarity or the museum or tourist image, is insulting.

> *James Stirling* 22.5.88

The days are over when the initials ARIBA were automatically assumed to mean 'always remember I'm a bloody architect.'

> *A voter in the RIBA presidential election* 14.12.86

All buildings spoil views. You cannot build a new building without somebody's view being impinged.

> *Michael Manser, President RIBA* 26.5.85

Bed and breakfast hotels must be Britain's equivalent to the shanty towns of the Third World.

> *Lord Scarman on the homeless* 11.10.87

To the average British farmer, organic farming is about as relevant as caviar and a flight on Concorde.

> *Oliver Walston* 15.1.89

FASHION

I know of only one civil servant who still comes to work in Whitehall in a bowler hat.

Sir Ian Bancroft, head of the Civil Service   14.12.80

Michael will look scruffy in whatever he wears.

Mrs Jill Foot   15.11.81

One good reason for wearing a bow-tie is that it lasts four times as long as an ordinary tie.

Mr Robin Day   13.1.80

Haute Couture should be fun, foolish and almost unwearable.

Christian Lacroix   27.12.87

Bra and pants are not a costume for a leading lady.

Ms Pippa Page   11.5.80

Never trust a man whose tie is habitually an inch below his collar.

Letter to The Times   5.7.81

A love of fashion makes the economy go round.

Liz Tilberis, new editor of Vogue   30.8.87

There is always a seasonal demand for French knickers just before Christmas.

Marks and Spencer spokesman 16.3.80

Expensive clothes are a waste of money.

Meryl Streep 7.11.82

I have more than one pair of trousers.

Sir Geoffrey Howe 7.12.82

Punk rock was the cultural phenomenon of the Seventies. Its greatest achievement was the way it made flared trousers unfashionable.

Tony Parsons 22.1.89

FOOD & DRINK

I often sit back and think 'I wish I'd done that' and find out later that I already have.

> *Richard Harris on drink*   22.5.88

If you want 100 per cent pure water, maybe you can have it – if you double the cost of providing it.

> *Nicholas Ridley*   25.10.87

It is not a civilised thing to eat freshly killed grouse.

> *Mr Egon Ronay*   17.8.80

With this so-called nouvelle cuisine there is nothing on your plate and plenty on your bill.

> *Paul Bocuse, the chef*   31.3.85

The French drink steadily and kill themselves with cirrhosis. The Scots drink in bouts and kill their neighbours.

> *Bill Sanders, Alcohol Study Centre, Paisley*   31.3.85

The right diet directs sexual energy into the parts that matter.

> *Barbara Cartland*   11.1.81

If someone asks for a soft drink at a party, we no longer think he is a wimp.

> *Edwina Currie*   11.12.88

I would not dare to change it. It is part of the soul of your country.

> *Antoine Riboud on the takeover of HP Foods*   10.7.88

If they want to get rid of me, they'll get rid of me through British Rail sandwiches.

> *Tony Benn*   30.9.84

I would walk miles for a bacon sandwich.

> *Princess of Wales*   3.4.88

We know more about what goes into a pair of socks than about what goes into our food.

> *Jonathan Aitken*   15.12.85

Do you not think champagne one of the greatest inventions of human beings?

> *Sir Sacheverell Sitwell*   21.11.82

Many children are suffering from muesli-belt malnutrition.

> *Professor Vincent Marks, nutritionist*   8.6.86

I mostly drink rather cheap wine and I like very simple food – cottage pie or fish cakes.

> *Roy Jenkins*   22.2.81

When it came to writing about wine, I did what almost everybody does – faked it.

> *Art Buchwald*   30.5.82

I don't have a sugar problem; I don't have cholesterol trouble. I just have a calorie problem.

> *Luciano Pavarotti*   10.8.86

What is traditional British cooking? We only have a few museum-pieces such as Lancashire hot pot.

Egon Ronay   14.2.82

A whiff of wine would knock me to the floor.

Princess of Wales   27.11.88

I'm very fond of my pigs; but I don't find it difficult to eat them.

The Archbishop of Canterbury   30.3.80

The diet of British schoolchildren is a disaster.

Geoffrey Cannon   6.4.86

You eat with your memory.

Egon Ronay   15.9.85

FOREIGN AFFAIRS

Read Jimmy Carter's memoirs? Surely you jest. Living through them was punishment enough.

> *Letter in Time*   31.10.82

When one is President of the Republic, one cannot say 'I'll wait and see.'

> *Giscard d'Estaing*   10.5.81

If you stay much longer you will go back with slitty eyes.

> *Duke of Edinburgh to English students in China*   19.10.86.

An Iranian moderate is one who has run out of ammunition.

> *Henry Kissinger*   26.7.87

Wouldn't it be nice for the British Government to have me eliminated?

> *Rev. Ian Paisley MP.*   22.11.81

If we follow violence the Chinese will find it easy to crush us. But if we use reason we can change the situation.

> *The Dalai Lama*   10.4.88

I arrived as a child; now I go back as an adult.

> *Mathias Rust*   7.8.88

If the UN would leave New York, nobody would ever hear of it again.

> *Mayor Koch of New York*   21.2.82

The army loves the people and the country.

> *Lt-General Henri Namphy, seizing power in Haiti*   6.6.88

We must fight this struggle with clean hands. The ANC has no policy of attacking people because they are a certain colour.

> *Oliver Tambo*   11.1.87

The attitude of all honest Afghans to Soviet troops is that of sincere hospitality and profound gratitude.

> *Tass*   16.3.80

I am not for change for change's sake.

> *P. W. Botha, Prime Minister of South Africa*   11.10.81

Megaphone diplomacy leads to a dialogue of the deaf.

> *Sir Geoffrey Howe*   29.9.85

All I would say is show me anywhere else where groups of people said to be mindless thugs and criminals produce 10 young men prepared to starve themselves to death for what they believe in.

> *Ken Livingstone on the IRA*   6.12.87

Our problem is that we are both romantics.

> *Ferdinand and Imelda Marcos*   15.3.87

In Poland everyone is a leader.

> *Lech Walesa*   15.3.87

He has to choose between Tambo and Rambo.

> *Rev Jesse Jackson on President Reagan and South Africa* 27.7.86

Irish Americans are about as Irish as black Americans are African.

Bob Geldof 22.6.86

In fundamental matters we Germans love confusion.

Mayor Manfred Rommel of Stuttgart 10.10.82

It's not that I don't have opinions, rather that I'm paid not to think aloud.

President Yitzhak Navon of Israel 9.1.83

The widow of Portsmouth is no different from the widow of Buenos Aires.

Richard Francis, managing director, BBC radio 16.5.82

If there are any shortcomings in implementing our open policy the main one is that China needs further opening.

Deng Xiaoping 25.1.87

Germans have a strong animosity towards enjoyment. They are wanting in lust for life. They just don't enjoy themselves when they eat.

Wolfram Siebeck, columnist 23.8.87

Not a franc, not a dollar, not a deutschmark, not a single yen.

Charles Pasqua on ransom for French hostages 8.5.88

Africa is talking to South Africa.

President P. W. Botha 9.10.88

Together, hand in hand, with our matches and our necklaces, we shall liberate this country.

Winnie Mandela 20.4.86

The Palestinian State is coming and its flag will fly over Jerusalem whether they like it or not.

Yasser Arafat 14.8.88

To say that peace is some sort of favour to Israel is absolute nonsense; the Arabs need peace just as badly as we do.

Shimon Peres 22.2.81

It seems that the British Government sees black people as expendable.

Bishop Desmond Tutu 22.6.86

I would have preferred to have had another father.

Rolf Mengele talking about his father, Joseph 22.6.86

For all practical purposes and into perpetuity there will never be a united Ireland.

Tom King 8.12.85

I've never used the word reform in my life.

Prime Minister Pieter Botha of South Africa 23.11.80

Italy is a poor country full of rich people.

Mr Richard Gardner, former US Ambassador to Rome 16.8.81

You and Reagan are kissing apartheid, embracing it.

President Kaunda to Sir Geoffrey Howe 27.7.86

It seems that the historic inability in Britain to comprehend Irish feelings and sensitivities still remains.

Charles Haughey 21.2.88

To have turned the other cheek would have meant that we should have become accomplices in making the world an even less stable place.

Archbishop of Canterbury on the Falklands 30.5.82

My generation, dear Ron, swore on the Altar of God that, whoever proclaims the intent to destroy the Jewish State or the Jewish people, or both, seals his fate.

Prime Minister Begin in a letter to President Reagan 8.8.82

What is sometimes forgotten is that the credibility and confidence of this government were built on five bloody years of terror. If the fear were lifted, the old aspirations would immediately spring up again.

Miklos Haraszki, Hungarian dissident 26.10.87

You won't force South Africans to commit national suicide.

President P. W. Botha 3.8.86

In spite of a few historical accidents – Joan of Arc, Fashoda, Waterloo – we have always admired our British friends' cool-headedness, fair play and skill at understatement.

France-Soir 6.4.80

I have not had major experience of talking with people once pronounced braindead, but I think we could be safe in saying he did not have great zip.

Sir Howard Smith, Ambassador in Moscow, on Brezhnev 11.9.88

One thing is quite clear: we are not going to have disloyal characters in our society.

Mr Robert Mugabe 24.4.80

My real problem is that I come from an anti-Nazi family.

President Kurt Waldheim 6.3.88

Stalinism is a wound which is still bleeding.

Anatoli Rybakov, novelist 27.11.88

Israel has nothing to apologise for.

Mr Begin 14.6.81

We are going to have peace here. My responsibility is to bring security for everyone. I don't like gunmen.

General Ghazi Kenaan, head of Syrian Military Intelligence in Lebanon 13.7.86

The British Government is an evil government as far as we are concerned in Northern Ireland.

> *Father Des Wilson of Ballymurphy* 26.6.83

Tyranny is colour blind and is no less reprehensible when it is committed by one of our own kind.

> *President Museveni of Uganda* 3.8.86

I'm not interested in the bloody system! Why has he no food? Why is he starving to death?

> *Bob Geldof* 27.10.85

It is not restraint when one State does not interfere in the internal affairs of another – it is the norm.

> *Chancellor Helmut Schmidt* 14.9.80

I see Nicaragua not only as a small country fighting a bully in the North but also in the front-line of trenches in a world-wide conflict.

> *Graham Greene* 26.4.87

There are no political prisoners here, the police are not armed and the Communist Party is smaller than my family.

> *Prime Minister Dom Mintoff of Malta* 17.5.81

Afghans have always worked out things together, when outsiders have left them alone. We will do so again.

> *Ex-King Zahir of Afghanistan* 27.3.88

I thought our difficulties went back 400 years. Now I've been told 700.

> *Margaret Thatcher after meeting the Taoiseach* 21.2.88

If you take a Frenchman out of his country for 50 years, he's still nothing but French.

> *Louis Jourdan* 5.6.83

The Palestinian State is coming and its flag will fly over Jerusalem whether they like it or not.

> *Yasser Arafat* 14.8.88

The conflict over the Falklands is a moment dislodged from its natural home in the late nineteenth century.

> *Lance Morrow* 11.10.82

In Britain Germany is well known, among other things like football and fast cars, for the excellence of its military officers down through history and the brilliance of its intellectuals.

> *Prince Charles* 8.11.87

As a trained diplomat, it was an aberration on my part.

> *Sir Geoffrey Harrison, on his affair with a Soviet Chambermaid* 1.3.81

I think the period of splits is past.

> *Yasser Arafat* 10.1.88

We have not closed down our parties, just suspended their activities.

> *General Kenan Evren, military ruler of Turkey* 5.4.81

I am a realist. No one can beat the Vietnamese in battle, not even the United States.

> *Prince Sihanouk* 6.2.81

Under the strictest, tightest sanctions, South Africa can chug along for a good many years where most of the front-line states won't last much longer than a couple of months.

> *Wilbur Smith, writer* 10.8.86

China will emerge as a tremendous economic and military power in the 21st century.

> *Japanese Institute of Foreign Affairs* 31.8.80

The cold war was not so terrible and detente was not so exalting.

> *Dr Henry Kissinger* 10.2.80

The Marxist analysis has got nothing to do with what happened in Stalin's Russia; it's like blaming Jesus Christ for the Inquisition in Spain.

> *Tony Benn* 27.4.80

Paisley has been, and remains a greater threat to the Union than the Foreign Office and the Provisional IRA rolled into one.

> *Mr Enoch Powell*   11.1.81

Whoever tries to climb over our fence, we shall climb over his roof.

> *President Saddam Hussein of Iraq*   30.7.80

I am not prepared to accept the economics of a housewife.

> *Jacques Chirac to Margaret Thatcher*   6.7.87

The justified yearning of citizens to live in a free environment, something which has become a matter of course in the twentieth century, cannot be stifled by crude violence.

> *Cardinal Tomasek, Primate of Czechoslovakia*   29.1.89

Our image has undergone a change from David fighting Goliath to being Goliath.

> *Yitzhak Shamir*   29.1.89

The Soviet Union has helped the people very much with humanitarian aid.

> *General Boris Gromov, Red Army commander in Kabul* 5.2.89

Whoever thinks of stopping the uprising before it achieves its goals, I will give him 10 bullets in the chest.

> *Yasser Arafat*   22.1.89

The whole imposing edifice of modern medicine is like the celebrated tower of Pisa – slightly off-balance.

>*The Prince of Wales* 19.12.82

Remember you can lose a lot of heat, on a cold night, through your head.

>*Edwina Currie* 25.9.88

It could be said that the Aids pandemic is a classic own-goal scored by the human race against itself.

>*Princess Royal* 7.2.88

I want to go to my grave as a complete human being – not part man and part pig.

>*Sir Michael McNair Wilson, MP* 7.8.88

My message to the businessmen of this country when they go abroad on business is that there is one thing above all they can take with them to stop them catching Aids and that is the wife.

>*Edwina Currie* 15.2.87

I don't smoke, so neither does my office staff.

>*Sir Yue-Kong Pao, Hong Kong shipping millionaire* 15.8.82

In the era of the permissive society people expected to be able to take a pill for everything.

> *Dr Heather Ashton*   21.2.88

If new-borns could remember and speak, they would emerge from the womb carrying tales as wondrous as Homer's.

> *Newsweek*   10.1.82

I had a caesarian myself. I know about it.

> *Mrs Thatcher, visiting a German gynaecological ward*   13.11.83

Instead of drinking Coca Colas, turn on the tap and drink what the good Lord gave us.

> *Edwina Currie*   13.11.88

Why do they get at the nurses?

> *Princess of Wales*   29.11.87

I'm an overweight athlete rather than a fat slob.

> *Robbie Coltrane*   19.4.87

I haven't had a puff since 26 August last year. I don't miss it and I feel better.

> *Fidel Castro on giving up smoking*   31.8.88

We are actually selling spaghetti to Italy, bulbs to Holland, brussels sprouts to Brussels.

> *Peter Walker*   18.10.81

I can still do the Charleston: Who the hell can lead a coup against me?

> *Lord Grade*   13.9.81

I don't think people are free if they're unemployed.

> *Peter Shore*   3.4.85

I am sick to death of Fleet Street. At times they act like lemmings.

> *TUC print committee chairman Bill Keys*   4.10.81

For all too many years people went to schools which despised the world of work and went to universities which totally rejected it.

> *Lord Young, Employment Secretary*   6.10.85

Capitalism without bankruptcy is like Christianity without Hell.

> *Frank Borman, Eastern Airlines chief*   9.3.86

I believe in benevolent, dictatorship provided I am the dictator.

> *Richard Branson, head of Virgin Records and the Virgin Atlantic airline* 25.11.84

Business only contributes fully to society if it is efficient, successful, profitable and socially responsible.

> *Lord Sieff* 30.8.81

Just as people can price themselves out of jobs, they can price themselves into jobs.

> *Sir Keith Joseph* 6.7.80

Dr Johnson could have said: When you know you are going to be privatised in a fortnight, it concentrates the mind wonderfully.

> *Mrs Thatcher* 10.10.82

We are jolly lucky to have all that oil.

> *Sir John Methven, Director General, CBI* 17.12.80

The future of Rowntree is in the hands of the money changers – the City Smarties.

> *David Williams, union leader* 12.6.88

An ideal world might mean no pay increases at all.

> *Sir Geoffrey Howe* 11.7.82

There is something about the British character that equates service with being servile.

> *Lord Young* 3.3.85

First of all the Georgian silver goes, and then all that nice furniture. Then the Canalettos go . . . In the ordinary working of the economy we are practically bankrupt save for oil. We are the Abu Dhabi of today.

> *Earl Stockton on privatisation* 10.11.85

The airline has been conducted in the past as though money grew on trees.

> *Sir John King, chairman, British Airways* 24.10.82

I am not going to be Minister of rubbish.

> *Richard Branson   20.7.86*

Get your tanks off our lawn.

> *Professor Roland Smith, chairman, House of Fraser   7.11.82*

We are keeping our tanks on the lawn.

> *Mr R. W. 'Tiny' Rowland, chief executive, Lonrho   7.11.82*

In the not-too-distant future, the notion of the annual pay increase must become as exceptional as it was novel a generation ago.

> *Sir Geoffrey Howe   24.10.82*

How many people in Britain recognise that we export as a percentage of our total production twice as much as the Japanese?

> *Sir Raymond Pennock, CBI   28.6.81*

I'll answer some of your questions, the more difficult ones will be answered by my colleagues.

> *Prof. Roland Smith, Chairman of British Aerospace, at their annual meeting   15.5.88*

A Government I helped in ways of great importance has shown me now no respect.

> *Mohamed Al-Fayed on the Department of Trade Inquiry into House of Fraser   19.4.87*

'Pan Am takes good care of you. Marks and Spencer loves you. Securicor cares . . . At Amstrad: "We want your money."'

> *Alan Sugar   3.5.88*

If there was a market in mass-produced portable nuclear weapons, we'd market them too.

> *Alan Sugar   14.9.86*

If there were a business Olympics, Britain would be winning quite a few gold medals.

> *Toshio Yamazak, Japanese ambassador to Britain   14.9.86*

We have got to take the gloves off and have a bare-knuckle fight.

Sir Terence Beckett, Director-General, CBI   16.11.80

No developed country can sustain one million unemployed for long periods of time without their minds becoming infected with a desire to topple the system.

Sir Frank Price, British Waterways   20.12.81

Overmanning has been replaced by unemployment, a change which is miserable in human terms in the short run but eventually carrying a potential for national advantage.

Mr John Biffen   16.8.81

What would have happened if Freddy Laker's firm had been in charge of London Transport?

Tony Benn   20.11.83

The sooner dirty and dangerous jobs in industry are carried out by robots, the happier we will all be.

Norman Tebbit   20.9.81

I have thousands of bad ideas all the time.

Clive Sinclair   20.2.85

By any standards this company is bankrupt and should be liquidated.

Ian MacGregor, Chairman, British Steel   14.12.80

In the days when the nation depended on agriculture for its wealth it made the Lord Chancellor sit on a woolsack to remind him where the wealth came from. I would like to suggest we remove that now and make him sit on a crate of machine tools.

Prince Philip   3.8.86

We are not over-burdened with people in politics who actually create businesses and create jobs.

Mrs Thatcher   13.9.81

You're not at a party two minutes before someone sidles up with a letter that's been lost in the post for a fortnight.

Sir William Barlow, Post Office Chairman 16.3.80

We worked too hard and too long to get women and kids out of the pits to put them back there now; and I bloody well won't have a woman down a mine so long as I'm president.

Joe Gormley 15.3.81

Train Crews have to perform miracles.

Les Felton, ASLEF executive member 18.7.82

We must have an enterprise culture, not a dependency culture.

Lord Young 6.3.88

If there are many applicants for a few jobs, the job is overpaid.

Milton Friedman 5.4.8

It is not the aim of this company to make more money than is prudent.

Marks and Spencer 10.5.87

If I had been a woman I would be constantly pregnant, because I simply cannot say no.

Robert Maxwell 7.8.88

We are moving into a period of massive demographic change. Our labour force will increase hardly at all during the 1990s.

Norman Fowler 17.7.88

The School of Hard Knocks, beloved of businessmen, is a somewhat unstructured comprehensive.

Lord Vaizey 19.6.83

The way to full employment is to allow jobs to occur.

Sir Keith Joseph 5.4.88.

LAW

Remember Mary Archer in the witness box? Your vision of her probably will never disappear. Has she elegance? Has she fragrance? Would she, without the strains of this trial, have radiance?

Mr Justice Caulfield 26.7.87

I don't think anyone would dispute that lots and lots of people are denied justice.

Sir David Napley 31.10.82

It's a job reserved for ageing lawyer politicians whose best days are far behind them. It's an antiquated position. It doesn't need to be reformed, it needs to be abolished.

Judge James Pickles on the office of Lord Chancellor 12.4.87

Sometimes even lawyers need lawyers.

Billy Carter 30.7.80

I was told to avoid stress, but that's a laugh in my job, how can you avoid it?

Sir Michael Havers, Attorney General 8.2.87

I think a person who lives here has a duty to understand the language.

> *Judge Malcolm Potter* 8.5.88

The poor darling – when she sacked me as Lord Chancellor she was in terrible distress.

> *Lord Hailsham on the Prime Minister* 29.5.88

I cannot resist saying that I regard our profession as one of the obstacles to national reform.

> *Lord Hailsham on lawyers* 14.9.86

Any ordinary person who is hearing these allegations is not in contempt of court discussing them with his wife or over dinner.

> *Lord Justice Dillon at the Spycatcher hearing* 24.1.88

Lawyers are honourable men and not a confederacy of smart Alecs.

> *Lord Edmund-Davies* 11.7.82

Justice without memory is an incomplete justice.

> *Elie Wiesel, Nobel Peace Prize winner, at the Klaus Barbie trial.* 7.6.87

You know our way of life. I'm afraid we drink perhaps half a dozen bottles over a weekend.

> *Judge Bruce Campbell* 4.12.83

When you have been a judge as long as I have, you get quite used to criticism.

> *Lord Denning* 3.2.80

There are defendants whom the judges are afraid of.

> *Alexander Solzhenitsyn* 29.5.83

Parliament makes the laws. The judiciary interprets them.

> *Lord Diplock* 10.2.80

Someone must be trusted. Let it be the judges.

> *Lord Denning* 23.11.80

You know, you can only perceive real beauty in a person as they get older.

Anouk Aimee 28.8.88

I think your whole life shows in your face and you should be proud of that.

Lauren Bacall 6.3.88

We live in a climate of insult.

British Rail chairman Sir Peter Parker 23.1.83

I would not say that the poor are poorer, except that they are more conscious of it.

Indira Gandhi 1.8.82

Something has changed with British. Their famous reserve has vanished.

Barcelona University psychologist 24.4.80

There's only one thing I miss. It's the smell of summer in the countryside in Cornwall.

Ronald Biggs 6.4.86

People's backyards are much more interesting than their front gardens, and houses that back on to railways are public benefactors.

Sir John Betjeman   6.3.83

Anyone who lives in this time is concerned with grottiness.

Peter Reading, poet   13.3.88

There's always a 'but' in my life.

Mrs Thatcher   17.5.81

I don't know exactly how many rooms there are. My best count is somewhere between 130 and 140.

George Howard on Castle Howard   14.2.82

Children today don't seem to have quite the same appetite for cruelty as they used to in the past.

Seth Trixon, Punch and Judy man   3.7.88

Arguably the only goods people need these days are food and nappies.

Sir Terence Conran   21.2.88

How did we break out of our ghettos and enter the mainstream of society and its privileges? Certainly not by riots and demonstrations.

Chief Rabbi Sir Immanuel Jakobovits   26.1.86

We are tending to be a lot more grasping and aggressive in our dealings with one another.

Rev. Ian Gregory, founder of the Polite Society   10.1.88

No society can survive without serious damage to its social fabric if self-interest is encouraged at the expense of other values.

The Bishop of Manchester   21.2.88

As the family goes, so goes the nation and so goes the whole world in which we live.

Pope John Paul II   7.11.86

I love entertaining. I have someone else to do the cooking, that's why.

> *Joan Plowright* 23.11.88

Council housing breeds slums, delinquency, vandalism, waste, arrears and social polarisation.

> *Geoffrey Pattie* 22.6.86

Belonging to a great clan makes an individual a better being, gives him a more fulfilled place in society.

> *Macdonald of Clanranald* 10.1.84

It resembles nothing more than a band of medieval brigands.

> *Douglas Hurd on the hippy convoy* 8.6.86

My mother always said to me: 'You know, if you had had a decent father you could have been a lawyer.

> *Walter Matthau* 4.9.88

There is something about going to sea. A little bit of discipline, self-discipline and humility are required.

> *The Duke of York* 9.10.88

There's never been a holiday like this. For £30 you can join the ranks of 40 paying prisoners of war at a chillingly realistic Colditz style concentration camp.

> *Great British Alternative Holiday Catalogue* 12.4.81

At 60 you might come back. At 70 they think you are ga-ga.

> *Sir Harold Wilson* 26.4.81

There's nothing the British like better than a bloke who comes from nowhere, makes it, and then gets clobbered.

> *Melvyn Bragg on Richard Burton* 25.9.88

There is nothing more ugly, I think, than a self-made man who worships his maker.

> *Bishop of Woolwich* 5.7.81

No society can survive without serious damage to its social fabric if self-interest is encouraged at the expense of other values.

> *The Bishop of Manchester* 21.2.88

I go abroad for my holidays.

> *Sir Henry Marking, Chairman, British Tourist Authority* 16.3.80

Life must be protected from becoming too artificial. We are going to have to think and work hard to protect ourselves against our own creations.

> *Lord Jakobovits, the Chief Rabbi* 3.1.88

I find it marvellous to actually get down to mucking out, milking cows, delivering calves and mending stone walls . . . somehow it straightens out your whole attitude to life.

> *Prince Charles* 17.8.86

In the middle ages people were tourists because of their religion, whereas now they are tourists because tourism is their religion.

> *Dr Robert Runcie* 11.12.88

Writing letters is a middle-class activity.

> *Robin McGregor, BBC audience researcher* 29.6.86

If anyone thinks £75,000 is a lot of money, he must be in a different world.

> *Mr Peter Cadbury* 18.1.81

Kids haven't changed much, but parents seem increasingly unhappy with the child raising phase of their lives.

> *Penelope Leach* 30.10.88

Absolutely nothing is exclusive now, except possibly White's.

> *Richard Compton Miller, diarist* 25.10.87

The nice thing about having relatives' kids around is that they go home.

> *Cliff Richard* 13.11.88

What to say to a docker earning £400 a week, owning a house, car, microwave and video and a small place near Marbella? You do not say 'Let me take you out of your misery, brother.'

Neil Kinnock (quoting Ron Todd)   4.10.87

In the old days you spoke of a person as being ill bred, or well bred, or cultivated. People read Henry James and Tolstoy and talked about them at dinner. Now you just talk about what you read in the papers.

Brooke Astor   12.6.88

Sociology is a lot of waffle. It is using a lot of words to cover up rather obvious remarks.

Lady Wootton   29.7.84

I answer 20,000 letters a year and so many couples are having problems because they are not getting the right proteins and vitamins.

Barbara Cartland   31.8.88

I am a father and no matter how much I try to convince myself toward the course of 'enlightenment' I know damn well that, put to the test, I'm what people would call a reactionary.

Neil Kinnock   31.8.86

Our willingness to put the kettle on is a facet of the English way of life which makes us attractive to tourists.

Michael Montagu, English   6.3.83

I was proud of the youths who opposed the war in Vietnam, because they were my babies.

Dr Benjamin Spock   8.5.88

In the immortal words of Frank Sinatra, 'If I drank as much and had as many women as I have said I have I would be in a jar in the Massachusetts Institute of Technology.'

Peter 'Taki' Theodoracopulous   15.6.88

It does seem to be true that the more you get the more you spend. It is rather like being on a golden treadmill.

> *Charles Allsop, commodities broker* 18.12.88

One change of country is enough for a lifetime.

> *George Mikes* 21.2.82

The British loathe the middle-aged and I await rediscovery at 65, when one is too old to be in anyone's way.

> *Sir Roy Strong* 3.1.88

What you learn on a farm is to put to use every resource you've got.

> *Mr George Howard, Chairman-designate, BBC* 13.7.80

I was on a basic £100,000 a year. You don't make many savings on that.

> *Ernest Saunders* 18.10.87

I want to give my kids the right values.

> *Jackie Collins* 18.10.87

The angries have grown old and got their goodies, and they don't know what to be angry about any more.

> *Rex Harrison* 21.4.88

An authentic Birmingham accent is something to be very proud of.

> *Keith Bowater, actor* 3.1.88

I haven't got the imagination to be frightened.

> *David Cowper, lone yachtsman* 27.4.80

Graciousness has been replaced by surliness in much of everyday life.

> *Margaret Thatcher* 1.5.88

£1500 a month is not what people need for living in central London.

> *Lord Gowrie, ex-Minister for the Arts* 8.9.85

Only Southerners can be fooled into believing that Northerners all live in out-of-work cloth-capped poverty.

> *Kenneth Clarke*   1.2.87

I will join the pensioners and create hell among the pensioners.

> *Mick McGahey on his future retirement activities*   22.6.86

It is only in our advanced and synthetic civilisation that mothers no longer sing to the babies they are carrying.

> *Sir Yehudi Menuhin*   4.1.87

At my age I must stop being a slave to my property.

> *Duchess of Bedford*   28.3.82

I spend hours watching faces. I get exhausted imagining what they are thinking.

> *Maurice Sendak*   30.10.88

Having a family is just like being in Kansas City.

> *Calvin Trilling*   4.1.81

If you can't be a bit different in Hampstead where can you be?

> *Anthony Earl-Williams, former Tory council candidate*   7.9.86

It's no good telling a man: 'Look, if you behave well, in 35 generations' time your son will have a slightly larger brain than you.'

> *Benny Green*   15.2.81

Population growth is the primary source of environmental damage.

> *Jacques Cousteau*   15.1.89

Never marry a man who hates his mother because he'll end up hating you.

Jill Bennett 13.9.82

I think English culture is basically homosexual in the sense that the men only really care about other men.

Germain Greer 24.4.88

I'd rather ask a man the time than a woman. I'd believe him.

Irene Handl 30.9.84

The most interesting man is the one who is not an easy lay.

Ms Jackie Collins 13.1.80

Men simply don't understand women.

Anna Ford, in an interview with Women's World 18.1.87

I like everything my beloved wife likes. If she wants to buy the top bit of St Paul's, then I would buy it.

Mr Denis Thatcher 7.4.85

More and more it appears that, biologically, men are designed for short, brutal lives and women for long miserable ones.

> *Estelle Ramey, physiology professor, Georgetown University*
> 7.4.85

I am exactly 50 years old, and have been now for 25 years.

> *James Cameron*   17.7.83

My wife is Arab and my mistress is French, and I maintain a relationship of betrayal with both of them.

> *Ben Jelloun, Prix Goncourt winner, on his bilingualism*
> 29.11.87

It is men who face the biggest problems in the future, adjusting to their new and complicated role.

> *Anna Ford*   4.1.81

The first time I married I was nervous, the second time was easier, and this time it was a canter.

> *Mr Stirling Moss*   30.3.80

No one asks a man how his marriage survives if he's away a lot.

> *Angela Rippon*   27.9.81

The secret of the success of our relationship is that we hardly ever see each other.

> *Paul Newman on his twenty-fifth wedding anniversary.*
> 30.1.83

Men play the game; women know the score.

> *Roger Woddis*   11.7.82

I feel like the luckiest man alive.

> *Dennis Stein, on his engagement to become Elizabeth Taylor's eighth husband*   16.12.84

There are many definitions of fidelity. Having a quick affair doesn't matter.

> *Trevor Howard*   4.1.81

When I'm married I want to be single, and when I'm single I want to be married.

> *Cary Grant*   3.5.81

Keeping the books has a wonderfully salutary effect on a man.

> *Enoch Powell*   14.2.82

Men are like buses. If you miss one, there's always another round the corner. But don't get caught at the wrong stop.

> *Wendy Henry, woman's editor, the Sun*   30.1.83

Why have hamburger out when you've got steak at home? That doesn't mean it's always tender.

> *Paul Newman on marriage*   11.3.84

I'm still trying to find the real Elizabeth Taylor and make her stand up.

> *Elizabeth Taylor*   11.3.84

I know I'm a small man but people notice me. I always command attention in a crowded room.

> *Peter Bruinvels, former MP.*   20.9.87

I'm just as romantic as the next guy, and always was.

> *John Lennon*   14.9.80

A man who is nothing values himself 10 times what he is; with a woman it is the other way round.

> *Naim Attallah*   22.3.87

Men are gentle, honest, and straightforward. Women are convoluted, deceptive and dangerous.

> *Erin Pizzey*   28.8.88

A man who has no faults has precious little.

> *Lord Shawcross*   30.6.85

We've been married six years and nowt comes between me and my Sunday dinner.

> *Yorkshire miner* 7.11.82

I'll cut his legs off and put him in a circus if he lets me down.

> *Mrs George Best on her husband* 24.2.80

The tragedy of men is that they live in this ghastly wasteland of secondhand jokes.

> *Jonathan Miller* 30.8.87

Behind every good man is a good woman – I mean an exhausted one.

> *Duchess of York* 6.9.87

I am seeking to do a favour for every woman in the kingdom.

> *Geoffrey Dickens MP.* 24.1.82

Those rich old men you sometimes see in hotels, like tortoises. They can destroy you with the power of their money. Everyone is browbeaten by them. They're killers.

> *Anthony Hopkins* 24.1.82

It's been very hard for me to lose my fear of men, and that's why I don't write about them very much.

> *Nell Dunn* 29.8.82

True love means never having to say you're sorry. Good divorce means never having to say you're broke.

> *Sylvester Stallone* 9.8.87

You can't stay married in a situation where you are afraid to go to sleep in case your wife might cut your throat.

> *Mike Tyson* 5.2.89

PHILOSOPHY

We do not necessarily improve with age: for better or worse we become more like ourselves.

> *Sir Peter Hall* 24.1.88

As I get older I seem to believe less and less and yet to believe what I do believe more and more.

> *Bishop of Durham* 6.11.88

No battle is worth fighting except the last one.

> *Enoch Powell* 30.5.82

Apart from the occasional saint, it is difficult for people who have the smallest amount of power to be nice.

> *Dr Anthony Clare* 10.8.86

Stalin I admired because he was the true representative of the Communist ideal. I knew that he was brutal but I thought that such great things were not possible without brutality.

> *Milovan Djilas* 29.6.86

People who never fantasise at all are often bland, colourless, matter-of-fact people, very rigid and repressed.

> *Dr James Council* 10.1.88

There must be some barriers that are not to be crossed, some limits fixed, beyond which people must not be allowed to go. The very existence of morality depends on it.

> *Mary Warnock* 22.7.84

There is no possibility of survival in our way of life.

> *Malcolm Muggeridge* 12.4.81

Everybody at times has fears of being a minority.

> *Archbishop of York* 14.2.88

Peace, after all, is not the least of our social services.

> *Lord Carrington, NATO secretary-general* 19.5.85

I think it is a tragedy when what I regard predominantly as pigmies can bring down a man like Cecil Parkinson.

> *Norman Tebbit* 20.11.83

Pleasant people are just as real as horrible people.

> *John Braine* 17.4.83

It's very pleasant to be back in these circumstances. But I do remember that room service was rather slow that night – I had to wait three and a half hours before anyone came.

> *Norman Tebbit on his return to the Grand Hotel* 31.8.88

If one is convinced that one's line of work and one's opinions are right, then one feels confident.

> *Kim Philby* 22.11.87

Undoubtedly some advertisements lead to fantasies. Life would be pretty intolerable without fantasies.

> *Lord McGregor, chairman of the Advertising Standards Authority* 31.8.88

Life gets harder the smarter you get, the more you know.

> *Katharine Hepburn* 25.10.87

It's now an admass society in which super-salesmen talk people into wanting more and more.

J. B. Priestley on his 86th birthday   14.9.80

I learned early in life that you get places by having the right enemies.

Bishop John Spong   31.7.88

I'm a 34-year-old whizzkid who has become a 35-year-old has-been.

David Stockman, US budget director   15.11.81

When you are younger you get blamed for crimes you never committed and when you're older you begin to get credit for virtues you never possessed. It evens itself out.

I. F. Stone   26.3.88

I can't stand people having the moodies.

Diana Moran, the exercise lady on BBC breakfast TV   30.1.83

It is hard to understand what man is capable of doing in the confusion of his mind and heart.

Pope John Paul II   23.11.80

I'm fascinated by power. Love to watch people get it, use it, then lose it.

Sally Quinn, author   3.5.87

I like to eat with nice people, to drink with nice people and to sleep with a clear conscience.

Lord Denning   18.7.82

There is no such thing as collective guilt.

President Kurt Waldheim   13.3.88

Hearts who seek quarrels understand nothing of God – and just as little about human needs.

Archbishop Glemp   5.9.82

You either get better or you die. To stick in a groove is an illness.

Leonard Bernstein   7.9.86

Nobody is ever truthful about his own life. There are always ambiguities.

Cary Grant   6.2.81

When you go in search of honey you must expect to be stung by bees.

President Kaunda of Zambia   9.5.82

There are few things more painful than to recognise one's own faults in others.

John Wells   23.5.82

An ounce of appreciation is worth a pound in money.

Sir Ian Bancroft, head of the Home Civil Service   12.7.81

Shyness is just egotism out of its depth.

Penelope Keith   3.7.88

Man treads upon his brother and silences him before he can ever draw one breath of this world's fresh air.

Christy Nolan   24.1.88

We love the wrong people at the wrong time for the wrong reasons.

Michael Korda   27.4.80

It is a good thing to follow the first law of holes; if you are in one, stop digging.

Denis Healey   8.5.88

Bearing children is in the end more important than anything else.

Piers Paul Read   6.1.85

What we believe is more important than our material existence, therefore warfare is a legitimate extension of values.

Dr Edward Norman   1.5.88

If you can't annoy someone, it does take a bit of the zest out of life.

Kingsley Amis   4.1.87

I've seen the American dream come true.

Senator 'Tip' O'Neill   26.10.87

I think some people do tend to fall in love with themselves at a certain time of life.

Actress Sian Phillips   26.10.87

It does no harm to throw the occasional man overboard, but it does not do much good if you are steering full ahead for the rocks.

Sir Ian Gilmour   20.9.81

How do we teach people to recognise that there is a dark side of man's psyche?

Prince Charles   7.9.86

Intellectuals are the most intolerant of all people.

Paul Durcan, poet   5.1.86

Chronology is the key to understanding everything.

Martin Gilbert   26.10.87

Someone who is not on good terms with the truth should take the consequences.

Dr Bruno Kreisky on President Waldheim   14.2.88

Start loving yourself and you're finished.

Terry Wogan   28.12.80

You know, by the time you reach my age, you've made plenty of mistakes if you've lived your life properly.

President Reagan   8.3.87

Moderation is a virtue only in those who are thought to have an alternative.

Henry Kissinger   24.1.82

Happiness is something I've hardly ever thought about.

> *Shirley Williams* 6.3.83

Thinking about the Eighties, I think first of antique Greek mythology. I think about Saturn – Saturn eating his own children.

> *Mr Günter Grass* 17.2.80

If you have the courage to love, you survive.

> *Maya Angelou* 16.8.87

A harsh truth is more salutary than a smooth evasion.

> *Abba Eban* 17.7.83

Most kids are born confident and then as they grow older it's knocked out of them.

> *Kim Wilde* 29.8.82

Everybody at times has fears of being a minority.

> *Archbishop of York* 14.2.88

The purpose of morality is to mitigate the harm that people may do to each other.

> *Baroness Warnock* 12.4.87

Every morning I read the obits in The Times. If I'm not there, I carry on.

> *William Douglas-Home* 16.8.87

Terrorism is armed propaganda.

> *Major-General Sir Frank Kitson, Commandant, Army Staff College* 13.1.80

Arrogance is not a proof of strength.

> *Lord Hailsham* 17.7.83

In today's terminology Karl Marx could be labelled a 'monetarist'.

> *Milton Friedman* 26.10.80

It seems that I have spent my entire time trying to make life more rational and that it was all wasted effort.

> *Sir Alfred Ayer*   17.8.86

As long as you can still be disappointed, you are still young.

> *Sarah Churchill*   12.4.81

Hell is when you get what you think you want.

> *Anthony Clare*   7.8.83

All of us distort our lives in the telling.

> *Bel Mooney*   24.7.83

The real problem in life is to have sufficient time to think.

> *Edward Heath, MP*   22.11.81

A learned man who is not cleansed is more dangerous than an ignorant man.

> *Ayatollah Khomeini*   6.7.80

Of course, history is always a kind of fiction.

> *John Carey, chairman of the Booker prize judges*   24.10.82

It's no use asking people if they regret things. It would be like asking King Lear if he regretted dividing up his kingdom.

> *Malcolm Muggeridge*   26.4.81

I am proud to have a son who died doing the job he loved for the country he loved.

> *Mr Harry Taylor, father of Lt Nicholas Taylor, shot down over the Falklands*   9.5.82

Only God creates, and all others pay.

> *John Boland, Irish Minister for the Public Service*   19.6.83

People laugh only when they feel secure.

> *Penelope Keith*   18.1.81

Everybody's going to die, so condolences should be sent, even between enemies.

> *President Mubarak of Egypt*   18.10.81

Show me a good loser and I'll show you a loser.

> *Paul Newman*   21.11.82

I have ceased being embarrassed about anything.

> *Harvey Proctor*   7.8.88

There is no English value which we should defend more vigorously than this tradition of tolerance.

> *William Whitelaw*   26.4.81

I can't stand moody people. You have to soothe them down all the time and be tactful.

> *Mrs Thatcher*   31.10.82

Once you have regrets you do everything in an orthodox way. And once you do everything in an orthodox way you don't get the highs and lows.

> *Jeffrey Archer*   12.4.87

It would be difficult for any country to have a set of laws making it illegal for people to discuss Aristotle.

> *Dr Anthony Kenny, Master of Balliol*   30.3.80

Love of one's country is not a cause.

> *Lord Annan*   15.5.88

The cliché 'charity begins at home' has done more damage than any other in the English tongue.

> *Bishop Trevor Huddleston*   14.9.80

One of the many pleasures of old age is giving things up.

> *Malcolm Muggeridge*   28.12.80

It makes you feel humble. It kind of makes you feel small.

> *Governor Dixy Lee Ray of Washington State, on the eruption of Mount St Helens* 1.6.80

Shaking hands and knowing are two different situations.

> *Frank Sinatra* 15.2.81

The thing is, 90 per cent of your worries are about things that won't happen.

> *Mrs Thatcher* 18.10.81

Truth is always duller than fiction.

> *Piers Paul Read* 12.4.81

The enemy of idealism is zealotry.

> *Neil Kinnock* 15.2.87

You can have too much of a good thing.

> *Nigel Lawson* 28.8.88

I was a sort of green; it was safe, it avoided confrontation. It was easier to save trees than people.

> *Albie Sachs on his youth* 6.11.88

People are very secretive creatures – secret even from themselves.

> *Mr John le Carré* 10.2.80

I like the idea of reincarnation, and it helps me to control my temper.

> *Miss Pat Phoenix* 6.4.80

The greatest problem about old age is the fear that it may go on too long.

> *A. J. P. Taylor* 1.11.81

There is a notion in the West that you own freedom. I think it is a very dangerous notion.

> *Dr Julius Tomin* 9.10.88

Happy the man who has nothing, because he has nothing to lose.

> *Keith Best, former MP.*   31.7.88

Tito said that the greatness of the people of a country can be assessed by how they stand up when they find themselves in difficult moments.

> *Mr Dusan Gligorijevic, President, Yugoslav League of Communists.*   11.5.80

Looking back over my life, everything seems to have happened by accident.

> *A. J. P. Taylor*   21.6.81

When you start unravelling traditional taboos it's like unravelling knitting. It's hard to stop.

> *Duke of Edinburgh*   31.5.81

I am a peace-loving person, but I am not a pacifist – there are some things worth dying for and human freedom could claim to be very high on the list.

> *Bishop Desmond Tutu, General Secretary, South African Council of Churches*   1.6.80

Don't you realise the enormous contempt the British working class has for do-gooders?

> *Professor Alan Walters*   28.12.80

I'm worried by privileged people who have no internal resources.

> *Candia McWilliam, novelist*   29.1.89

You come into the world alone, you go out alone. In between it's nice to know a few people, but being alone is a fundamental quality of human life, depressing as that is.

> *Helen Mirren*   29.1.89

ı ne only consensus in Britain is that every trade union, institution, profession and organisation, from the Crown to the unemployed, believes that it should have more money.

Jo Grimond   18.10.81

I think Tory MPs are a lot more romantic. They possibly dress better than Labour Members and our insults are certainly more gentlemanly.

Hugo Summerson, MP.   11.12.88

A manifesto is issued to get votes and is not to be taken as gospel.

Lord Denning   15.11.81

I don't think radicalism and being sensible are incompatible.

Joan Ruddock   26.4.87

Stop in God's name before you leave our country in ruins.

Cardinal Thomas O'Fiaich to the IRA   6.11.83

Only one person in the world alters the vote of an MP – his wife

Joe Ashton, MP.   15.11.81

Communism stops only when it encounters a wall.

> *Mr Alexander Solzhenitsyn*   17.2.80

Examining one's entrails while fighting a battle is a recipe for certain defeat.

> *Denis Healey*   19.6.83

It is important never to commit yourself in politics to anything that is utterly, indelibly factual.

> *Francine Gomez, French politician*   9.3.86

I have made it clear that the period of coalitions, necessary though it was, is now over. We are on our own.

> *Paddy Ashdown*   31.7.88

It was not a defeat, I was merely placed third in the polls.

> *Bill Pitt, Liberal candidate for Croydon NW.*   26.7.81

If the old mould is being broken, it looks like being replaced by a very familiar model, produced in a traditional political kiln belonging to Backbite and Bollocks.

> *Cyril Smith*   10.1.82

Communists should be the first to be concerned about their people and country and the last to enjoy themselves.

> *Zhao Ziyang*   27.3.88

Being the leader of the Labour Party is the worst job in Britain.

> *John Prescott*   4.9.88

After nine years in opposition we have not put ourselves in a position where people trust us, and I regard that as politically incompetent.

> *Merlyn Rees*   4.9.88

If you had listened to me on defence you wouldn't be where you are now.

> *James Callaghan to John Prescott over tea*   15.3.87

I was allowed to ring the bell . . . for five minutes until everyone was in assembly. It was the beginning of power.

> *Jeffrey Archer on his school days*   20.3.88

Starvation in the midst of plenty is more than fiscal lunacy, it is a diagnosis of political paralysis.

> *Mayor Kevin H. White of Boston, Mass.*   10.1.82

I expect nothing from British politics. They have been very kind to me in the past.

> *Roy Jenkins*   15.6.80

The House of Lords is for the first time more representative of the people than is the House of Commons.

> *Lord Kennet*   3.7.83

I still love winning. I have a distinct aversion to losing.

> *Norman Tebbit*   27.2.86

I'd love to be minister for motivation.

> *Jeffrey Archer*   6.6.88

I frequently liken my job to going for a ride. I mount the saddle every day at 2.30.

> *Bernard Weatherill, Speaker of the Commons*   17.4.88

The Commons is hardly a den of passion.

> *Anna McCurley, MP.*   10.5.87

Politics come from man. Mercy, compassion and justice come from God.

> *Terry Waite, in Libya*   3.1.85

So long as the Labour Party remains the main party of Opposition, it remains true that it is only a matter of time before Britain becomes an Eastern Bloc-style, so-called democratic republic.

> *Lord Hailsham*   15.2.87

I don't think that modesty is the outstanding characteristic of contemporary politics, do you?

> *Edward Heath*   4.12.88

Anybody who enjoys being in the House of Commons probably needs psychiatric help.

> *Ken Livingstone*   31.1.88

The Labour Party's always in great shape.

> *Alex Kitson*   22.11.81

It is not the title that counts. I will be the same shape in the bath as before.

> *Mr George Thomas*   3.7.83

I think I have found it the best job in the world, being Prime Minister.

> *Margaret Thatcher*   7.8.88

Brothers, I'm on my way before the remains of Karl Marx are disinterred from Highgate Cemetery and reburied in Parliament Square.

> *Lord Cudlipp*   22.11.81

You cannot set up a new party overnight.

> *David Owen*   1.2.81

Never before has the Labour Party offered the country a defence policy of such recklessness. It has talked of occupation – a defence policy of the white flag.

> *Margaret Thatcher*   31.5.87

Where human beings are directly affected small steps are infinitely more important than big words.

> *Willy Brandt*   5.10.80

My passion exists but it is controlled.

> *David Owen*   31.5.87

I did not enter the Labour Party 47 years ago to have our manifesto written by Dr Mori, Dr Gallup and Mr Harris.

Tony Benn 19.6.88

People think we do not understand our black and coloured countrymen. But there is a special relationship between us.

Elize Botha, wife of South Africa's President 3.5.87

I don't accept that politics is a power struggle, completely unethical and unprincipled.

Edward Heath 26.1.86

You see the word in print, that terrible M; the R, the X, and everybody shivers.

Hans Werner Henze on being a Marxist. 20.3.88

The more the misery, the merrier the militants.

Norman Tebbit 10.10.82

When I'm sitting on the Woolsack in the House of Lords I amuse myself by saying 'Bollocks' sotto voce to the bishops.

Lord Hailsham 11.8.85

For the past few months she has been charging about like some bargain basement Boadicea.

Denis Healey on Mrs Thatcher 7.11.82

I plan to be the Gromyko of the Labour Party for the next 30 years.

Denis Healey 3.2.84

The Emperor Nero, we are told, fiddled while Rome burned. But at least he noticed that Rome was burning.

Sir Ian Gilmour 13.10.85

Landslides, on the whole, don't produce successful governments.

Francis Pym 22.5.88

You four-eyed git, I will see you outside.

Tony Banks, MP, speaking in the Commons 11.3.84

The British constitution reserves all its ultimate safeguards for a non-elected èlite.

> *Tony Benn* 13.9.81

I have nothing against Hampstead; I used to live there myself in the days when I was an intellectual. I gave that up when I became Leader of the House.

> *Norman St John-Stevas* 13.9.81

Her real reason for objecting to sanctions is to defend British interests. Those interests will go up in flames.

> *President Kenneth Kaunda* 25.5.86

If the party is not a party of self-discipline and of will to win you might have to look for someone else.

> *Neil Kinnock* 15.3.81

It really is the Great Adventure!

> *David Owen on politics* 6.3.88

I would like to tell you the secrets of what happened in the last Cabinet – but I haven't been in as many Labour Cabinets as Tony has.

> *Michael Foot* 6.3.88

Margaret Thatcher doesn't smoke, but if she did you would hear the clash of gold-plated Ronsons every time she put a fag in her mouth.

> *Conservative MP* 20.9.81

Nowhere in the world has radical social change ever been accomplished by Parliament.

> *Peter Tatchell* 16.1.83

I would eat Mr Kinnock for breakfast.

> *Norman Tebbit* 15.12.85

Part of the problem is that many MPs never see the London that exists beyond the wine bars and brothels of Westminster.

> *Ken Livingstone* 22.2.87

I believe Mr Benn has completed his long march to the lunatic asylum of politics.

    Richard Cottrell, MEP   16.2.86

There are lots of ways to get socialism, but I think trying to fracture the Labour Party by incessant contest cannot be one of them.

    Neil Kinnock   7.2.88

A man's nation is the nation for which he will fight.

    Enoch Powell   22.2.81

The British obsession with background had a great impact on driving me to the top.

    John Moore, Transport Minister   24.8.88

Dogmas, theories and ideologies are disastrous weapons of government.

    Francis Pym   4.12.83

People can say what they want in the Labour Party.

    Michael Foot   25.1.81

You can compromise and compromise and compromise again and destroy the party you love.

    David Owen   25.1.81

For us the British Parliament is as foreign as the French Parliament, the Japanese diet or the American Senate.

    Gerry Adams, MP.   15.1.84

I don't believe either man could have played poker. Their faces gave it away.

    Lord Bullock on Ernest Bevin and Winston Churchill
    13.11.83

I think there are very real doubts as to whether Mr Kinnock is capable of raising himself to the level of a parliamentary under secretary of state.

    Norman Tebbit   10.4.88

The only safe pleasure for a parliamentarian is a bag of boiled sweets.

>   *Julian Critchley MP.*   13.6.82

The amateur in politics is the person who is always sure he knows the result of the next General Election.

>   *Enoch Powell*   6.2.81

Government's don't retreat, they simply advance in another direction.

>   *Geoffrey Rippon, MP.*   15.11.81

Britain has invented a new missile. It's called the civil servant – it doesn't work and it can't be fired.

>   *General Sir Walter Walker*   15.3.81

If disabled Pakistani lesbians wanted to form a section of the Labour Party, I do not see how you could stop them.

>   *Tony Benn*   21.7.85

Elections are so healing.

>   *Tony Benn*   5.4.81

Above any other position of eminence, that of Prime Minister is filled by fluke.

>   *Enoch Powell*   8.3.87

There is no such thing as sound and healthy power-sharing. If you share power, actually you lose it; you lose control.

>   *Dr Andries Treurnicht*   19.10.86

The present world atmosphere is not healthy. Things are decided by force, guns and money.

>   *The Dalai Lama*   20.9.87

There were two revolutions in the early Twentieth Century. One was the revolution of morals and the other was the revolution of money.

>   *Mr William Rees-Mogg*   14.6.81

In England life is not governed by ideas, ideas are born from life.

President von Weizsacker of West Germany   8.6.86

Extremism and conservatism are contradictions in terms.

Francis Pym   19.6.83

The idea that I have served my political life in rolling pastures or leafy suburban avenues, which some newspapers seem to suggest, is ludicrous.

Mr Roy Jenkins   14.6.81

They travel best in gangs, hanging around like clumps of bananas, thick skinned and yellow.

Neil Kinnock on Tory critics   22.2.87

Democracy is a school with endless classes, permanent education.

Shimon Peres   17.5.81

There is no longer a set of social democratic ideas that will work.

Lord Vaizey   7.12.80

We'd like a by-election once a fortnight.

Manager's secretary, Firgrove Inn, Warrington   19.7.81

Some of our best politicians are unable to form a grammatical sentence of more than 10 words.

Daily Telegraph   20.2.83

The great teachers of Marxism – Marx himself, Lenin and Trotsky – were all prepared under certain conditions to go to the courts.

Militant   21.11.82

I would never do anything to deride the profession of politics – although I think it is a form of madness.

Lord Home   7.8.83

This country has never had as good a time as it has today . . . We've never had it so good for the 87 per cent of us who are working.

Lord Young   1.6.86

No one's argument is advanced by abuse.

> *The Speaker*   1.11.81

I remember crying quite uncontrollably in Portsmouth. My public persona was one of total control, but internally I was totally wrought up.

> *David Owen on the break up of the SDP*   14.8.88

Don't underestimate the ability of party politicians to find alibis.

> *Michael Heseltine*   11.10.81

Frankly, actually, surprisingly, no.

> *Lord Whitelaw on any regrets at not becoming Prime Minister*   17.1.88

I just have a great belief that people in this country don't expect us to dash into elections at the first opportunity.

> *Margaret Thatcher*   11.1.87

We don't chase off to some ultra-Leftist Disneyland where insurrection and general strikes are supposed to bring capitalism crashing to the ground.

> *Neil Kinnock*   11.1.87

He never consults me on anything.

> *Denzil Davies, MP, resigning as Labour Defence spokesman*   19.6.88

The Left should always avoid personality politics like the plague and have no heroes and no scapegoats.

> *Tony Benn*   27.7.86

To stay in No. 10 most Prime Ministers would eat their own grandmothers.

> *New Society*   27.7.86

The rule of practice for serious politicians is 'Read, read, read.' One can never read enough.

> *Enoch Powell*   9.1.83

Almost every senior Minister goes through a period when, for whatever reason, the Press get at him.

John Moore   24.1.88

There is a tide in the political history of this country and that tide is flowing with us.

Dr David Owen   26.6.83

Everything that is most beautiful in Britain has always been in private hands.

Nicholas Ridley   17.1.88

Wayward woman.

Mr William Hamilton, MP, on Princess Margaret   6.4.80

Parliament itself would not exist in its present form had people not defied the law.

Mr Arthur Scargill   6.4.80

A centre party, if it's something just pushed around between the others, is not right.

Roy Jenkins   14.12.80

The House of Commons is terribly outdated, an old man's club with too much spare-time boozing.

Mrs Shirley Williams   22.11.81

I have always been interested in Third World issues more than in domestic issues.

Glenys Kinnock   4.12.88

I did not go into politics to be a kamikaze pilot.

John Biffen   1.3.81

I pay £1,500 a year in rates and for that I expect my dustbin to be collected from my door.

Michael Parkinson   25.5.86

I can still remember the day when I encountered my first Conservative, a shock all the greater in that it coincided with the crisis of puberty.

      Professor Gwyn Williams, historian of Merthyr Tydfil   30.8.81

I think Dr Owen would accept that he is not the easiest of people to work with.

      David Steel   13.7.86

You don't have power if you surrender all your principles – you have office.

      Ron Todd   19.6.88

We shall be bloody to them. They will be bloody back. And then we shall just be even more bloody.

      British Cabinet Minister on the EEC, quoted in the Guardian   9.3.80

I want to say goodbye, farewell to this funny movement, this fallacy, this international falsehood.

      Colonel Qadhafi on the Non-Aligned movement   7.9.86

It is no exaggeration to describe plain English as a fundamental tool of government.

      Margaret Thatcher   13.3.88

Karl Marx is arguably the most important person who has ever lived in London.

      GLC Arts Committee chairman Tony Banks   6.3.83

It confirms my belief that this is not the time to merge the two parties.

      Dr David Owen, MP, about the Liberal Assembly vote on nuclear defence   29.8.86

Build on the great open site of human freedom: the homes, the families, the values, the enterprises – in a word, the good society.

      Margaret Thatcher   8.6.86

I was the original SDP – on my own.

> *Lord Shawcross*   19.6.83

He who wields the knife never wears the crown.

> *Michael Heseltine*   16.2.86

The Labour Party won't die. It will metamorphose.

> *Margaret Thatcher*   5.6.83

I've always thought a stuff-'em-all party would poll a lot of votes.

> *David Penhaligon, MP (Lib).*   25.10.81

I have never considered joining the Tories.

> *David Owen*   15.5.88

In the world I live in nobody ever feels that their view has been fairly presented.

> *Tony Benn*   4.11.82

Socialists make the mistake of confusing individual worth with success. They believe you cannot allow people to succeed in case those who fail feel worthless.

> *Kenneth Baker*   13.7.86

The trouble with Labour is that if the TUC says jump, the party jumps.

> *Eric Hammond*   12.6.88

You have to eat an elephant slowly, mouthful by mouthful. That's what we are doing.

> *Benazir Bhutto*   17.8.86

I won't be sat on and I won't have someone speak for me.

> *Edwina Currie*   14.9.86

During the lean years of disarmament, when very little appeared to be happening, the Society of Friends and the Communist Party, self-effacing people, did an enormous amount to keep the flag flying.

> *Mgr Bruce Kent to the British Communist Party congress*
> *16.11.83*

If there is any emergence of a fourth party in this country, it is the task of the Liberal Party to strangle it at birth.

> *Mr Cyril Smith.* 18.1.81

The Conservative Party will never govern Britain from the South of England. It will govern as a national party or not at all.

> *Michael Heseltine, MP.* 8.2.87

The Civil Service always hopes it is influencing Ministers towards the common ground.

> *Sir Anthony Part, former permanent secretary to the*
> *department of industry* 7.12.80

Revolutions are celebrated when they are no longer dangerous.

> *Pierre Boulez* 15.1.89

PRESS

I am leaving for philosophical reasons.

> *Libby Purves, on resigning the editorship of Tatler*   10.7.83

Journalists belong in the gutter because that is where the ruling classes throw their guilty secrets.

> *Gerald Priestland*   22.5.88

One of the reasons I decided to publish my diaries was that I never leak.

> *Barbara Castle*   15.6.80

Now I'm ashamed to be English.

> *Kevin Keegan*   15.6.80

I told the Prince that Murdoch was an ogre and he replied: 'Ah yes, I knew his father.'

> *Mr Anthony Holden*   21.3.82

In the goldfish bowl of media publicity, there is much waterweed.

> *Michael Shea*   20.11.88

It is well known that all Fleet Street editors take a vow of chastity upon assuming office, and a vow of poverty too.

Stewart Steven, Mail on Sunday editor 29.5.88

Anyone who gives an interview to the Press gives up a portion of their life and soul.

Lesley Garner 31.7.88

I've been in this business 25 years and whenever some MP is given a going over by the Press, usually for all the right reasons, they start trying to get a privacy bill.

Nigel Dempster 22.1.89

You're a hero one day and menace the next. These things pass.

Rupert Murdoch 14.2.88

Give someone half a page in a newspaper and they think they own the world.

Jeffrey Bernard, columnist 1.6.86

A good journalist has a lot of shoe leather, a conscience, and the ability to see the world from the wolf's point of view.

Fred W. Friendly 26.7.81

It is not our fault so much of what appears is gloomy.

Mr David Nicholas, Editor, ITN 2.3.80

I think I'd go to prison for the Sun, but not for The Times.

Rupert Murdoch 6.1.85

Many journalists have fallen for the conspiracy theory of government. I do assure you that they would produce more accurate work if they adhered to the cock-up theory.

Bernard Ingham, press secretary to the Prime Minister 17.3.85

I had a good Press this weekend. No one mentioned me.

Lord King 21.2.88

Positivity is news. Negativity is not news.

> *Justin Nyoka, Zimbabwe Director of Information* 25.10.81

I don't know how good she is for the country, but she's good for me.

> *Cartoonist Wally Fawkes (Trog) on Mrs Thatcher* 30.3.80

Oh, No, No, you would not dream of changing them at all.

> *Mr Rupert Murdoch speaking of Times Newspapers* 18.1.81

Photographers are the most loathesome inconvenience. They're merciless. They're the pits.

> *Paul Newman* 25.10.81

It is going to take a lot of negotiation and a lot of time before we get Fleet Street really on its feet.

> *Rupert Murdoch* 12.7.81

I still believe that, if your aim is to change the world, journalism is a more immediate short-term weapon.

> *Tom Stoppard* 12.7.81

I don't read the Press. I read responsible literature.

> *Princess Michael of Kent* 30.11.86

I am a businessman, not a moralist. Porn is in the eye of the beholder.

> *Andrew Cameron of United Newspapers* 6.9.87

I'm proud to be a muckraker when the cause is good.

> *Geoffrey Pinnington, Editor of the Sunday People, on its centenary* 18.10.81

People seem to think they are doing me a favour in allowing me to take on something that is losing £13 million a year.

> *Rupert Murdoch* 15.2.81

Journalism is a sure way of using up your intellectual capital.

> *John Maddox, Editor, Nature* 22.6.80

I don't like naked women.

> *Clive Thornton, chairman, Mirror Group Newspapers*
> 15.1.84

Anybody who is rung up by more than one reporter thinks they're being hounded!

> *Sir Woodrow Wyatt* 19.1.86

The Press is at a very low ebb – perhaps the lowest for half a century.

> *Lord Deedes* 17.1.88

Our Press is absolutely free. In fact I feel sometimes it's even worse than your Press.

> *Prime Minister Rajiv Gandhi at the Washington National Press Club* 23.6.85

I don't see why I should do anything for them, they never do anything for me.

> *Princess of Wales, on Press photographers* 25.10.87

The popular press rolls people down a trivial slope. It's not patronising to want people, as they get older, to grow wiser.

> *Sir Roy Shaw* 30.8.87

Photo-journalism is dead.

> *Mark Boxer* 22.2.87

Great newspapers should not change hands as though they are packets of tea.

> *Lord Goodman* 22.2.87

Nobody west of Exeter ever reads the New Statesman.

> *Arthur Marshall* 27.9.81

We are leaving behind not just history and tradition but a nightmare almost entirely of our own making.

> *Lord Deedes on the exodus from Fleet Street* 14.2.88

The participation of the media in the lobby system is a public disgrace.

> *Sir Frank Cooper* 16.3.86

I would not want anyone looking at me to think that this man is a thick, stupid, illiterate yob.

> *Derek Jameson, former editor of three national newspapers* 19.2.84

Blood sport is brought to its ultimate refinement in the gossip columns.

> *Bernard Ingham* 9.2.86

I expect in the fullness of time to become the Denis Thatcher of the SDP.

> *Peter Jenkins* 7.3.82.

RACE

When blacks are out of control they are completely out of control. The way to get them under control is to use force, more force than they can take.

Theunis Swanepoel, 1976 Soweto commander 22.6.86

I really don't think bingo will provide a stable economy for our tribe.

Wilma Mankiller, new Chief of the Cherokee Indians 22.12.85

At every general election the Tory Party cannot resist playing the race card and they are doing it again now.

Gerald Kaufman 22.3.87

They can proscribe black sections, but they will never keep the issue of black representation out of the Labour Party.

Bernard Grant 19.4.81

There are some people who think that only folk with black faces have got feelings.

Prime Minister Muldoon of New Zealand 4.10.81

Last week we sold two gollies to a Rastafarian couple.

> *Assistant in Hamley's* 24.10.82

Deep-rooted racial prejudice probably takes about five years of concentrated psychotherapy to dispel.

> *Chief Inspector Ian McKenzie, Metropolitan Police Training School* 16.1.83

South Africa will not allow the double standards and hypocrisy of the Western world, even in the application of legal principles, to stand in the way of our responsibility to protect our country.

> *President P. W. Botha* 25.5.86

I marvel at the resilience of the Jewish people. Their best characteristic is their desire to remember. No other people has such an obsession with memory.

> *Elie Wiesel* 17.7.88

A Labour Government will maintain firm immigration control, there's no doubt about that.

> *Gerald Kaufman* 15.6.88

There are only five million Scots in Scotland, and 20 million throughout the world. Their impulse is to leave.

> *Sean Connery* 24.10.82

We want to forget about race.

> *Oliver Tambo* 2.11.86

It could never be a correct justification that, because the whites oppressed us yesterday when they had power, that the blacks must oppress them today because they have power.

> *Mr Robert Mugabe* 30.3.80

The soil of our country [South Africa] is destined to be the scene of the fiercest fight and the sharpest struggles to rid our continent of the last vestiges of white minority rule.

> *Nelson Mandela* 15.6.80

RELIGION

In the beginning was the Word. It's about the only sentence on which I find myself in total agreement with God.

> *Mr John Mortimer QC.* 1.7.84

I don't want to bore God.

> *Orson Welles on why he doesn't pray* 28.3.82

Sunday is not for sale.

> *Lord Tonypandy on Sunday Trading* 8.12.85

Dissent from church doctrine remains what it is, dissent. As such it may not be proposed or received on equal footing with the church's authentic teaching.

> *Pope John Paul II* 20.9.87

All the time I feel I must justify my existence.

> *Prince Charles* 5.9.82

They drive me mad – I can't bear them.

> *Mrs Rosalind Runcie on church bells* 13.3.83

Only God can put everything right.

> *Lord Hailsham*   13.7.80

Organised religion is making Christianity political rather than making politics Christian.

> *Sir Laurens van der Post*   14.11.86

No one gives a fig about the Ten Commandments any more.

> *Lord Chief Justice Lane*   14.11.86

Britain's condom culture desperately needs the Church's call to chastity and fidelity.

> *John Gummer*   14.2.88

I'm divorced twice but I would prefer to die a bad Catholic than have the Church change to suit me.

> *Richard Harris*   25.10.87

If I really believed that the Church of England came out of the loins of Henry VIII I could be as free as I liked about making changes, but I do not believe that.

> *Canon Peter Boulton on women priests*   1.3.87

St Teresa of Avila described our life in this world as like a night at a second-class hotel.

> *Malcolm Muggeridge*   6.3.83

Can the fact that Our Lord chose men as his Twelve Apostles be lightly dismissed?

> *Bishop of Winchester*   10.7.88

There are times and occasions when it would be marvellous to have a wife.

> *Cardinal Hume*   6.2.81

He had the attitude of a medieval. He thought that the way to be virtuous was to withdraw from life and take care of the soul.

> *I. F. Stone on Socrates*   18.9.88

The Pope receives movie stars, Communists and atheists. But he does not like to meet with critical Roman Catholic theologians.

> *Hans Kung*   7.8.83

It will undoubtedly be necessary to wait several years for Rome to find once more its 2,000 year old tradition.

> *Archbishop Marcel Lefebvre*   6.6.88

Catholics and Communists are fighting together against the death squads in El Salvador, against the Contras in Nicaragua and against General Pinochet in Chile.

> *Graham Greene*   22.2.87

I feel that I want to kneel and kiss Mother Teresa's feet.

> *Dr Robert Runcie*   16.2.86

We must reject a privatisation of religion which results in its reduction to being simply a matter of personal salvation.

> *Dr Robert Runcie*   17.4.88

Part of the problem of the Catholic Church is that at the highest level it is conservative with a small 'c' and a large 'C.'

> *Bruce Kent*   8.3.87

We have now stopped being a Christian country.

> *Bishop of Durham*   29.3.87

Our protection depends, I believe, on the mystical power which from time immemorial has been called God.

> *Prince Charles*   28.2.82

Clearly God is not exclusively male. He (She?) must reflect all that is female.

> *Bishop of Durham*   29.8.86

The world is not a place where good is rewarded and evil punished.

> *Canon Colin Semper, head of BBC religious broadcasting* 4.1.81

You have riches and freedom here but I feel no sense of faith or direction. You have so many computers, why don't you use them in the search for love?

> *Lech Walesa* 18.12.88

Christ never promised a 'no-risk' pilgrimage.

> *Archbishop of Canterbury* 17.5.81

I'll be glad when the Lord calls me to heaven. I get tired down here sometimes.

> *Billy Graham* 17.1.88

I believe I have demonic forces opposed to me wherever I preach.

> *Dr Billy Graham* 3.2.80

I'm not defying anybody. I'm obeying God.

> *Archbishop Desmond Tutu* 11.9.88

I reacted against organised religion at university. I suppose everyone goes through that stage.

> *John Habgood, Archbishop-elect of York* 10.7.83

Londoners look on God and the Church with more disfavour than people anywhere else in England.

> *Tom Houston, director, the Bible Society* 10.7.83

The English are probably the most tolerant, least religious people on earth.

> *Rabbi David Goldberg* 30.3.80

Such persons are often good, conscientious and faithful sons and daughters of the Church.

> *Cardinal Hume, on Catholics who use contraceptives* 30.3.80

If you go to a Russian church the people you see are mainly old and mainly women, but the same is true of the Church of England.

> *Archbishop of York* 1.6.86

If you become holy, it is because God has made you so. You will not know it anyway.

> *Cardinal Hume* 10.1.84

If the devil can quote scripture, surely a bishop can quote Lenin.

> *Bishop of Chester* 22.6.80

There is a serious need in the Christian churches to affirm strongly to today's world our common belief in the existence of the Evil One.

> *Cardinal Suenens* 21.9.90

The General Synod has made a bit of a mess of the Lord's Prayer.

> *Bishop of Durham* 12.4.81

Has it occurred to you that the lust for certainty may be a sin?

> *Dr John Habgood* 11.12.88

I cannot see how God can possibly sort us out when we get to the gates of heaven or hell.

> *Barbara Woodhouse* 18.10.81

Someday the authorities in Rome will thank us for having preserved this tradition, its doctrine, its faith, for the greater glory of God.

> *Archbishop Marcel Lefebvre* 3.7.88

What sort of God are we portraying and believing in if we insist on what I will nickname 'the divine laser beam' type of miracle as the heart and basis of the Incarnation and Resurrection?

> *Bishop of Durham* 13.7.86

There is always a danger in Judaism of seeing history as a sort of poker game played between Jews and God, in which the presence of others is noted but not given much importance.

> *Rabbi Lionel Blue* 29.8.82

The question of the rights of women to hold secular office is a quite separate matter and should not in any way be connected to or paralleled with the question of women's ordination.

> *Cardinal Willebrands* 8.6.86

There is, mercifully, still something so magical about Sunday morning, a feeling that not all the secularising of the day can destroy.

Mary Whitehouse   15.8.82

Only a socially just society has the right to exist.

The Pope, in Brazil   6.7.80

Without centuries of Christian antisemitism, Hitler's passionate hatred would never have been so fervently echoed.

Dr Robert Runcie   13.11.88

With Judaism we have a relationship which we do not have with any other religion. You are our dearly beloved brothers and, in a certain way, it could be said that you are our elder brothers.

Pope John Paul II   20.4.86

Lambeth Palace is rather difficult to make into a home.

Mrs Rosalind Runcie   15.6.80

History has been made in this church today. By me.

Rev Sylvia Mutch, the first woman to conduct a marriage ceremony in the Church of England   22.3.87

A belief in God and a belief in astrology cannot be reconciled.

Rev Jerry Falwell   22.3.87

God wants us to be rich and comfortable.

Walter Hoving, Chairman of Tiffany's   9.1.83

I used to be in favour of women priestesses but two years in the Cabinet cured me of them.

Norman St John-Stevas   16.5.82

Jesus said love one another. He didn't say love the whole world.

Mother Teresa   2.3.80

There is far more religious faith in Russia than in England.

Graham Greene   15.6.80

Read the Bible, Work hard and honestly. And don't complain.

> *Billy Graham in China* 24.4.88

Christianity is the most materialistic of all the world's religions.

> *Lord Soper* 13.6.82

One good point about Marxism is that it recalled Christianity to its responsibilities.

> *Bishop Desmond Tutu* 26.4.81

I believe that God created man. I object to teachers saying that we come from monkeys.

> *Rev. Ian Paisley* 27.4.80

I recognise that Buddhism exists and that Chichester district council is not going to change Buddhism into Christianity overnight.

> *Councillor Peter Luttman-Johnson* 30.3.80

France, eldest daughter of the Church, are you faithful to the promises of your baptism?

> *The Pope* 15.6.80

Jesus Christ was not a Conservative. That's a racing certainty.

> *Eric Heffer* 20.2.83

Christ called as his Apostles only men. He did this in a totally free and sovereign way.

> *Pope John Paul II* 25.9.88

She seems a very nice girl.

> *The Queen on Koo Stark*   31.10.82

It is very tragic that elderly people cannot afford high electric and fuel bills.

> *Princess of Wales*   16.3.86

Lady Diana Spencer is a direct descendant of Genghis Khan.

> *Professor Juan Balonso, Madrid genealogist*   1.3.81

Actually sitting down and thinking is a sweat.

> *Prince Charles*   16.11.80

Life is one big act. You may be nervous, but you don't show it.

> *Prince Edward*   4.12.83

The increase of the 'black' economy shows that people do not, once they are freed of their companies, their unions and to a certain extent, their Government, shirk the idea of work.

> *Prince Charles*   22.11.81

I feel positively delighted and frankly amazed that Di is prepared to take me on.

> *Prince Charles*   1.3.81

Royalty puts a human face on the operations of government.

> *Archbishop of Canterbury*   20.6.80

The night before the [royal] wedding I hardly slept a wink. My wife Mary and I were already up at dawn.

> *Sir Harold Wilson, writing in Stern magazine*   20.6.80

He's the only one who knows how to work the video.

> *The Queen on Prince Andrew*   11.8.85

If you find you are to be presented to the Queen, do not rush up to her. She will eventually be brought around to you, like a dessert trolley at a good restaurant.

> *Advice in the Los Angeles Times*   6.3.83

These wretched babies don't come until they are ready.

> *The Queen*   7.8.88

I have never been anywhere really. I came from school, went to work and then got married.

> *Princess of Wales*   31.3.85

I don't want you here – now sod off!

> *Princess Anne to a photographer*   11.1.87

I wish I had been Bob Geldof.

> *Prince Charles*   21.2.88

I'm a working girl. I haven't got time to gad about all over the country.

> *Sarah Ferguson*   23.2.86

I'm as thick as a plank.

> *Princess of Wales*   25.1.87

I've got a better background than anyone else who's married into the Royal Family since the war, excepting Prince Philip.

> *Princess Michael of Kent* 18.12.88

Leave her alone, for God's sake.

> *Buckingham Palace spokesman on the Princess of Wales*
> 21.11.83

I simply wasn't their idea of a princess.

> *Princess Anne* 18.12.88

What worries me is that we are going to end up as a fourth-rate country.

> *Prince Charles* 1.12.85

I thank God I am British.

> *Prince Charles* 28.6.81

What you want is a 'Dynasty' production where everybody can see what we do privately.

> *Prince Philip* 15.6.88

I do not see why I should be handicapped by the wife.

> *Mark Phillips* 14.2.88

I don't think the Queen does interviews with people and I can quite understand why.

> *Sir Robin Day* 15.2.81

I'm no playboy. What is a playboy anyway?

> *Prince Andrew* 24.7.83

I promise you there is nobody here.

> *Prince of Wales to photographers at Sandringham* 18.1.81

Five per cent? Five per cent? You must be out of your minds.

> *Prince Philip on the birthrate in the Solomon Islands*
> 24.10.82

The thing I might do best is be a long-distance lorry driver.

> *Princess Anne*   24.8.80

I do not play with a Ouija board. I don't even know what a Ouija board is.

> *Prince Charles*   27.10.85

Waste of bloody time. I'm sorry I came.

> *Willie Hamilton, MP, on his tea with the Queen*   4.7.82

Only the other day I was inquiring of an entire bed of old-fashioned roses forced to listen to my ramblings, on the meaning of the universe as I sat cross-legged in the lotus position in front of them.

> *Prince Charles*   20.11.88

I have done my best.

> *Princess Margaret*   11.5.80

Being a daughter you tend to get further adrift from the family than the boys.

> *Princess Anne*   20.12.81

Oh, you rotter!

> *Duchess of York to a weighing machine*   5.2.89

He does not want to become King in an atmosphere where there would be no-go areas in our cities.

> *Rod Hackney, architect, after dining with Prince Charles* 27.10.85

No party has a monopoly over what is right.

> *Mikhail Gorbachov*   2.3.86

As the ancient Greeks say: 'Everything flows, everything changes.'

> *Mikhail Gorbachov*   22.5.88

If he changes the Army as well as the Party, then what is stable?

> *General John Galvin on Gorbachov*   4.12.88

Farewell, unwashed Russia, the country of slaves!

> *Nicholas Daniloff (quoting Lermontov)*   5.10.86

The future of Russia is indissolubly linked to the Church and the revival of Christianity.

> *Alexander Ogorodnikov*   26.4.87

The vast majority of Russians only want to travel abroad to get an impression of what it is like and then come home.

> *Yevgeny Yevtushenko*   7.11.86

The Soviet people want full-blooded and unconditional democracy.

> *Mikhail Gorbachev*   13.6.82

The Soviet Union would remain a one party nation even if an opposition party were permitted – because everyone would join that party.

> *President Reagan*   13.6.82

The Union of Soviet Socialist Republics is not just a country, but an empire – the largest and probably the last, in history.

> *Time*   22.6.80

Our achievements leave class enemies restless.

> *President Brezhnev*   12.4.81

We give all our cosmonauts the title of Sportsman of the Soviet Union.

> *Vladimir Popov, vice-president, Soviet Olympic Organising Committee*   30.7.81

The Russians are not madmen.

> *Lord Home*   25.5.80

We can't solve our current and future problems if we do not say the whole truth about the past.

> *Yevgeny Yevtushenko*   8.6.86

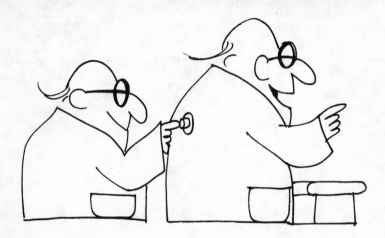

Should we force science down the throats of those who have no taste for it? Is it our duty to drag them kicking and screaming into the twenty-first century? I am afraid that it is.

Sir George Porter 7.9.86

Science is not an absolute to which all things have to be subordinated and eventually sacrificed, even the dignity of man.

Cardinal Joseph Ratzinger 15.3.87

You mustn't think scientists are stupid.

Sir Monty Finniston 16.1.83

You are distracting us with unnecessary nagging. Get rid of all those unnecessary staff at mission control. We have our instructions and are doing our best.

Yuri Romanenko, record-breaking Soviet cosmonaut, to ground control 3.1.88

It is a remarkable fact that, genetically, we are closer to the chimpanzee than, say, a horse is to a zebra.

Richard Leakey 10.5.81

Science may be described as the art of systematic oversimplification.

Sir Karl Popper   1.8.82

Can I say, as someone who is lucky enough to be a father of five young children, there is not any way in which I could support any form of energy that is a danger to them and their families.

Peter Walker on nuclear energy   8.6.86

SEX

They are going to turn us all off sex pretty soon if they don't stop.

Jane Russell on topless models   9.3.86

Once a week there will be striptease shows and the old boys won't want to die because they will be having so much fun.

Cynthia Payne on her plans to open an old people's home
13.7.86

Most women know that sex is good for headaches.

Dr Tom Smith   1.11.87

However much men say sex is not on their minds all the time, it is most of the time.

Jackie Collins   19.7.81

Personally I know nothing about sex because I've always been married.

Zsa Zsa Gabor   16.8.87

We hope people will learn to love condoms. In the past people like Casanova had lots of fun with their condoms.

David Cox, producer of a TV Aids programme   1.3.87

I first became an adultress to the sound of Mozart.

> *Jacquetta Hawkes* 5.10.80

My view is that we are all bisexual.

> *Ken Livingstone* 29.3.87

I said 10 years ago that in 10 years time it would be smart to be a virgin. Now everyone is back to virgins again.

> *Barbara Cartland* 12.7.87

All that mattered to me was the smell of his tweed jacket and his thick hair falling across my face.

> *Shirley MacLaine, describing an affair with a Labour MP*
> 5.6.83

A man who is old enough to die for his country is old enough to be able to decide who to sleep with.

> *Joint Council for Gay Teenagers* 12.4.81

I have always been discriminating in my choice of lovers, but once in bed I am like a slave.

> *Britt Ekland* 13.7.80

Only the English and the Americans are improper. East of Suez everyone wants a virgin.

> *Barbara Cartland* 25.1.81

All women should marry younger men. After all, men reach their sexual prime at 19 and women can reach it at 90.

> *Penelope Keith* 16.10.83

Lusting is what keeps a lot of men going into old age.

> *Dustin Hoffman* 1.5.88

France is the only place where you can make love in the afternoon without people hammering on your door.

> *Barbara Cartland* 28.10.84

I cannot imagine a Christian society in which divorce, abortion, sexual relationships before marriage and homosexuality are tolerated.

> *The Pope in Holland*   18.5.85

When people say, 'You're breaking my heart,' they do in fact usually mean that you're breaking their genitals.

> *Jeffrey Bernard*   18.5.85

Many women, and I agree with them, think there is some connection between the rising tide of sexual crime and Page Three.

> *Clare Short, MP.*   16.3.86

I like naked ladies – one at a time, in private.

> *Bernard Levin*   27.10.85

It seems to me quite impossible for any court to find that the refusal by a wife to have sex more often than once a week is unreasonable.

> *Lord Justice Ormrod*   7.12.80

The first thrill of adultery is entering the house. Everything there has been paid for by the other man.

> *John Updike*   6.1.85

The days of being promiscuous are over.

> *Elizabeth Taylor*   31.5.87

If I am elected I won't be the first adulterer in the White House. I may be the first one to have publicly confessed.

> *Gary Hart*   17.1.88

I may commit adultery again if God moves me to it.

> *Preacher Philip Dring of the Assembly of God Mission*
> 7.12.80

There are a lot more interesting things in life than sex, like gardening or reading.

> *Jean Alexander, actress*   17.8.86

Just because I've got blonde hair and big boobs people think I'm dumb.

> *Samantha Fox* 8.6.86

I think we're returning to a moral view which smells strongly of carbolic.

> *Dr Alex Comfort, 'Joy of Sex' author* 3.5.87

The more sex becomes a non-issue in people's lives the happier they are.

> *Ms Shirley MacLaine* 21.9.80

I know it does make people happy, but to me it is just like having a cup of tea.

> *Cynthia Payne on her interest in sex* 8.2.87

I'm not against homosexuals as people.

> *Rev Tony Higton* 8.11.87

The strongest possible piece of advice I would give to any young woman is: Don't screw around, and don't smoke.

> *Edwina Currie* 3.4.88

SHOW BUSINESS

For 10 years I was the devil. Now suddenly I'm an angel.

> *Yoko Ono* 16.8.81

Humour? It is something that thrives between man's aspirations and his limitations.

> *Victor Borge at 75* 10.1.84

A tour is great fun for a while. But it's like sex – you don't want to do it all the time.

> *Mick Jagger* 22.11.81

Generally I feel very fortunate. It's been a good life. I mean, if you're going to be born and be in a rock-and-roll band, you may as well be in the Beatles.

> *George Harrison* 22.3.87

We are still a duet. John is doing what he can upstairs. I do what I can down here.

> *Yoko Ono* 1.11.81

People should be aware that they are more likely to lose their control and self-restraint in a country-and-western bar than anywhere else.

> *James Schaefer, anthropologist*   4.12.88

This band has no politics, we're just pissed off.

> *Hoxton Tom, bassist of the 4-Skins*   12.7.81

He could be a manoeuvring swine, which no one ever realised.

> *Paul McCartney on John Lennon*   10.11.85

To work as hard as I've worked to accomplish anything and then have some yo-yo come up and say, 'Take off those dark glasses and let's have a look at those blue eyes' is really discouraging.

> *Paul Newman*   5.10.86

If you sit down doggedly to be 'funny' first, last and all the time, the chances are you'll end up in the soup.

> *Barry Took*   13.3.83

You can't name me one great comic who is under 40.

> *Jimmy Tarbuck*   29.8.86

I've been thrown out of better places than this.

> *Peter Langan, restaurateur, after a misunderstanding at the Savoy Hotel*   27.7.86

People come up to me, shake my hand, shout 'Walkies' and scream with laughter.

> *Barbara Woodhouse, in Los Angeles*   6.9.81

The nicest people can't be funny and witty the whole time. Totally witty people are quite tedious.

> *Helen Lederer, comedian*   27.12.87

I won't be photographed with that over-made-up tart.

> *Princess Margaret, on Boy George*   3.6.84

I wish I had a dollar for every time I sang 'Climb Every Mountain.'

> *Jessye Norman*   14.9.86

Some of my best leading men have been dogs and horses.

> *Elizabeth Taylor*   22.2.81

I really could have been a brain surgeon because I was a very bright child.

> *Cilla Black*   4.1.81

We've been up, we've been down, we've been in love, we've been out of love, we've been every which way.

> *Paul McCartney on his marriage*   24.8.88

Age is not a friend of women, it is the enemy, but it can be a good ally of an actress.

> *Simone Signoret*   23.6.85

Once you've been a comedian nobody takes you seriously any more.

> *Eric Sykes*   24.8.88

SPORT

The goal was scored a little bit by the hand of God, another bit by the head of Maradona.

> *Diego Maradona*   29.6.86

You think my run-up is long? You should have heard my speeches!

> *Wes Hall, Barbados Tourist Minister and former fast bowler* 8.11.86

It's one of the real sports that's left to us: a bit of danger and a bit of excitement and the horses, which are the best thing in the world.

> *The Queen Mother on horse racing*   29.3.87

Getting sacked is just part of the football scene.

> *Mr Malcolm Allison*   12.10.80

The Soviet people don't like the Olympics because all the food is going to foreign visitors.

> *Ilya Dzhirkvelov, KGB defector*   25.5.80

It seems everything I do people are going out of their way to knock down.

> *Ian Botham*   23.3.86

Comprehensives don't produce any cricketers.

> *Jim Laker* 16.6.85

The business of winning medals and doing well in international sport is the icing on the cake, but not the fruit of sport.

> *Duke of Edinburgh* 6.6.88

Cheating has now become absolutely necessary in professional cricket today.

> *Hasib Ahsan, manager of the Pakistan touring team* 16.8.87

Can snooker live without me?

> *Alex Higgins* 30.11.86

I think tennis has missed me – I don't think there is much question about that.

> *John McEnroe* 10.8.86

It is nice to say that I'll enjoy my birthday party completely sober.

> *George Best on reaching 40* 25.5.86

We are close to having a side capable of taking on the world.

> *Bobby Robson* 24.8.88

They've been cheating us for 37 years – and by us I mean other teams as well as England.

> *Mike Gatting on Pakistan* 7.2.88

I played hard and drank reasonably hard on occasions without making a fool of myself.

> *Sir Gary Sobers* 6.6.88

The thing with sport, any sport, is that swearing is very much part of it.

> *Jimmy Greaves* 21.2.88

Anyone who can't score from a penalty needs shooting.

> *Graham Rix* 18.5.80

Chess is too valuable a commodity for the human race.

> *Florencio Campomanes, World Chess Federation president*   10.8.86

I did not put a rose down my flies. I did not call Raman Subba Row, the manager of the England party in India, a wog. I did not ask for Ken Barrington's first-class ticket when he died.

> *Geoffrey Boycott*   28.2.82

When the gun goes, you become a different human being.

> *Mr Allan Wells, Olympic 100 metres champion*   16.8.81

I am not saying women umpires are not so good. It's just harder to get upset with a lady in the chair.

> *John McEnroe*   21.6.81

I was driving on crowd power. They put five seconds on me.

> *Nigel Mansell, after winning the British Grand Prix* 19.7.87

There is no such thing as a football hooligan. They are all just hooligans.

> *Mr Brian Clough*   21.9.80

Just because we're England, it doesn't mean we have a divine right to go all over the world beating other countries.

> *Bobby Robson*   20.11.88

It will take something of the magnitude of a war to stop the Olympic Games.

> *Sir Denis Follows*   30.3.80

I dunno. Maybe it's that tally-ho lads attitude. You know, there'll always be an England, all that Empire crap they dish out. But I never could cop Poms.

> *Jeff Thomson, Australian fast bowler*   26.10.87

I wasn't happy when the umpire told the spectators to be quiet. That only encourages them to make more noise.

> *John McEnroe*   27.6.82

I never really knew what it meant to communicate with somebody else.

> *Jimmy Connors* 7.6.87

Women are always asking for photographs of me leaning over the snooker table. It's my bottom they want to look at.

> *Steve Davis* 16.5.82

My back will always give me problems.

> *Mr Denis Thatcher on golf* 23.11.80

I ain't no great showman, I ain't going to get flash and talk the ass off a donkey.

> *Frank Bruno* 20.7.86

Brilliant. We did our bit for English football.

> *A soccer fan on his return from the Amsterdam riot* 17.8.86

If you are involved in any kind of hunting operation on a sensible scale, the hunter is the only person who wants that species to survive.

> *Duke of Edinburgh* 10.1.84

It was more like a football terrace than Lord's.

> *Mr Ian Botham* 19.7.81

If this is world football, I'm glad to be going home.

> *Alex Ferguson, Scotland's manager, after the match with Uruguay* 15.6.88

It may sound arrogant but I feel I have been the best 800 metres runner in the world since 1978.

> *Sebastian Coe* 31.8.88

Sport is the most unifying influence in the world today.

> *Sir Denis Follows, Chairman, British Olympic Association* 9.3.80

Top tennis is overpaid.

> *Sue Barker*   23.5.82

The underarm delivery was an act of cowardice. It was appropriate that the Australian team was wearing yellow.

> *Prime Minister Robert Muldoon of New Zealand*   6.2.81

I don't think the country would accept me as a gentleman.

> *Ian Botham*   11.3.84

All I think about is winning that bleedin' title.

> *Frank Bruno*   15.1.89

What young men and young ladies get up to in the evenings during a Test Match doesn't worry me a bit. That's the least of my worries.

> *Ted Dexter*   5.2.89

If the African nations ever succeeded in their plan for one British team in the World Cup, I'd vote Tory. That is how serious it is. I ask you, a load of spear throwers trying to dictate our role in world football.

> *Brian Clough*   15.2.87

People have a herding instinct. If a guy does not drink and goes off to practise or have dinner they think you are weird. You are not. You are different.

> *Geoffrey Boycott*   7.6.87

You can't decide how you're going to play a ball before it's delivered.

> *Ian Botham*   30.8.81

Do you know the difference between involvement and commitment? Think of ham and eggs. The chicken is involved. The pig is committed.

> *Martina Navratilova, the tennis star*   5.9.82

Who writes your script?

> *Graham Gooch to Ian Botham*   24.8.88

Girls are a distraction and can easily cost points.

> *Boris Becker, tennis star*   15.6.88

My own feeling is that fish do not feel pain, but I think they can feel panic.

> *Don Thomson, Salmon and Trout Association*   10.1.84

Tennis players are very sensitive people.

> *John McEnroe*   26.6.83

It was about par for a rugby dinner – from what I can remember.

> *Colin Smart, England prop forward*   28.2.82

How am I going to live without cricket?

> *Ian Botham*   1.6.86

I've never tolerated phoneyness in anyone and there's a lot of it at Wimbledon.

> *Mr John McEnroe*   16.8.81

It is extraordinary, but there are more horses in this country today than there were in the 1850s.

> *Angela Rippon*   31.8.80

THATCHERISM

There is no such thing as society. There are individual men and women and there are families.

Margaret Thatcher   1.11.87

It is quite clear to me that the Tory Party will get rid of Mrs Thatcher in about three years time.

Sir Harold Wilson   23.11.80

I do not think I could take more than another 10 years of such years as this.

Mrs Thatcher   1.8.82

We will resist the calls for easy options. Ulysses, you will remember, resisted the siren voices and came safely home to harbour.

Mrs Thatcher   28.2.82

We had to fight the enemy without in the Falklands. We always have to be aware of the enemy within, which is more difficult to fight and more dangerous to liberty.

Mrs Thatcher   22.7.84

The spread of personal ownership is in harmony with the deepest instincts of the British people. Few changes have done more to create one nation.

> *Nigel Lawson* 24.1.88

We shall not perish as a people even if we get our money supply wrong – but if we get our human relationships wrong, we shall destroy ourselves.

> *Archbishop of Canterbury* 19.7.81

Our past has caught up with us.

> *Margaret Thatcher* 14.9.80

I think I have become a bit of an institution – you know, the sort of thing people expect to see around the place.

> *Margaret Thatcher* 19.7.87

She is a dominating person, as all Prime Ministers should be expected to be, but she is not domineering.

> *William Whitelaw* 29.5.83

She is the only Prime Minister I have known who is prepared also to moonlight as Leader of the Opposition.

> *Brian Walden, on Mrs Thatcher* 17.4.83

I am extraordinarily patient, provided I get my own way in the end.

> *Mrs Thatcher* 4.11.82

I only hope I've got my mother's knack of dealing with awkward questions.

> *Carol Thatcher* 7.3.82

If people just drool and drivel they care I turn round and say: 'Right, I also like to see what you do.'

> *Margaret Thatcher* 14.6.87

We must have an enterprise culture, not a dependency culture.

> *Lord Young* 6.3.88

The thing I notice is that I tend to look at things much more logically than my colleagues.

> *Mrs Thatcher* 16.3.80

If you are going from A to B you do not always necessarily go in a straight line.

> *Mrs Thatcher* 4.12.80

Patience is not one of my obvious virtues.

> *The Prime Minister* 3.2.80

Though we run the risk of being labelled as hard-hearted reactionaries for doing so, I believe that we should more fully appreciate the achievements of the Victorian age.

> *Peter Brooke, Conservative Party Chairman* 16.11.88

In another five years I will have been in 11½ years, then someone else will carry the torch.

> *Mrs Thatcher* 17.11.85

I cannot stand the people who said: 'Your duty is to relieve poverty' and when you have done it, turning around and saying: 'You belong to a materialist society'.

> *Margaret Thatcher* 4.9.88

The Prime Minister should go and read her history books, starting from the Pilgrimage of Grace.

> *Mr Michael Foot* 14.12.80

Austerity is philanthropy in Britain today.

> *Sir Terence Beckett, director-general, CBI* 7.11.82

There is no definition of the poverty line.

> *Mrs Thatcher* 17.7.83

It was then that the iron entered my soul.

> *Mrs Thatcher, on her time in Mr Heath's Cabinet* 27.3.83

With regard to opinion in the Thatcher household, the Prime Minister does not have a monopoly.

> *Mrs Margaret Thatcher* 22.6.80

In Margaret Thatcher's Britain, we are all on our own.

> *Roy Hattersley* 3.7.88

We must see to it that the country never has to make the choice between being divided but rich, or united but poor.

> *Francis Pym* 3.7.83

There are good times very much in prospect.

> *Margaret Thatcher* 25.1.87

You don't have to do that to me, my dear – I'm only in politics.

> *Margaret Thatcher to a curtseying shop assistant* 8.11.87

There can be no U-turns.

> *The Prime Minister* 15.6.80

I'll stay until I'm tired of it. So long as Britain needs me, I shall never be tired of it.

> *Mrs Thatcher* 21.2.82

Gain all you can, save all you can, give all you can.

> *Margaret Thatcher (quoting John Wesley)* 29.5.88

She really is a woman just like my mum.

> *Cliff Richard on the Prime Minister* 21.8.88

The poll tax is Thatcherism taken to its ultimate absurdity.

> *John Smith* 10.4.88

There have to be some opportunities for today's *nouveaux riches*, so I am not impressed by the case of the *anciens pauvres*.

> *Nicholas Ridley, on the sale of stately homes* 27.11.88

When Mrs Thatcher says she has a nostalgia for Victorian values I don't think she realises that 90 per cent of her nostalgia would be satisfied in the Soviet Union.

> *Peter Ustinov*   20.9.87

Let me say this – if you want someone weak you don't want me.

> *Margaret Thatcher*   2.3.86

She's shouted at me once or twice, but she shouts at everyone. When I retired she was very kind.

> *Sir Douglas Nass on Mrs Thatcher*   13.11.83

We now have no alternative but to accept a reduction in the country's standards of living.

> *Mrs Thatcher*   16.11.80

No one would remember the Good Samaritan if he'd only had good intentions. He had money as well.

> *The Prime Minister*   13.1.80

Everything that is most beautiful in Britain has always been in private hands.

> *Nicholas Ridley*   17.1.82

Do you remember what Queen Victoria said? 'Failure – the possibility does not exist.'

> *Mrs Thatcher*   11.4.82

Some young people used to say to me, 'There are not any rules any more.' They are crying out for a set of rules and standards by which to live.

> *Margaret Thatcher*   10.1.88

Our policies are perfectly right. There will be no change.

> *Mrs Thatcher*   31.8.80

I don't really know what a wet is.

> *Mr William Whitelaw*   23.11.80

I think, historically, the term 'Thatcherism' will be seen as a compliment.

> *Margaret Thatcher* 13.10.85

If you press her nicely, she will respond, but if you threaten to knock her block off, she will respond by knocking your block off.

> *Joe Gormley, on his wife and Mrs Thatcher* 21.6.81

If money from the Contingency Fund is spent once, it cannot be spent twice.

> *Mrs Thatcher* 23.5.82

We don't just sack a chap for one mistake.

> *the Prime Minister on Mr Jim Prior* 2.3.80

I don't want to have anything to do with Mrs Thatcher.

> *Robert Maxwell* 27.7.86

We have become a grandmother.

> *Mrs Thatcher* 5.3.89

It's not the job of the TUC to bring down Governments.

> *Len Murray* 1.3.81

We all of us should stop away from work. We should ask the public to join us and continue to stay away for the sake of our railway industry.

> *Mr Ray Buckton, General-Secretary, ASLEF* 7.9.80

We cannot negotiate under duress.

> *Eddie Shah* 4.12.83

What the system pays doctors, politicians and senior managerial staff should also be paid to miners.

> *Arthur Scargill* 11.7.82

I have long been of the opinion that if work were such a splendid thing the rich would have kept more of it for themselves.

> *Bruce Grocott, MP.* 22.5.88

If the kamikaze pilots were to form their own union, Arthur Scargill would be an ideal choice for leader.

> *Jimmy Reid* 17.1.88

These strikes just aren't worth it.

> *Mr Terry Duffy*   30.3.80

You must be living in cloud-cuckoo land if you think it could knock me sideways.

> *Arthur Scargill*   13.3.83

They may, in the fullness of time, even canonise me and make me a saint.

> *Mr Derek (Red Robbo) Robinson*   24.2.80

The occupation of tea lady cannot by any stretch of the imagination be described as hazardous.

> *Mr Justice Comyn*   31.10.82

The money spent on strikes was one of the best investments we have made.

> *Sir Peter Parker, BR chairman*   25.7.82

One of the main things that distinguishes democracies from dictatorships is the right to go on strike.

> *Len Murray*   6.3.83

They can take our money but they can't take our dignity.

> *Sam McCluskie*   8.5.88

It is difficult to go on strike if there's no work in the first place.

> *Lord George-Brown*   24.2.80

Women should not worry too much about size. They should be happier with themselves.

> *Selina Scott*   22.3.87

In the decades to come it will be extremely hard for two perfectly equal people to have a successful marriage in the traditional sense.

> *Grace Lichenstein, New York author*   1.3.81

I've always felt that English women had to be approached in a sisterly manner, rather than an erotic manner.

> *Anthony Burgess*   31.7.88

A 40-year old may well be smarter than a 23-year-old. I wonder how many men would object to Joan Collins as their secretary?

> *Diane Cornish of Brook Street Bureau*   3.1.88

Marriages not infrequently break up because the more compliant partner eventually feels compelled to re-assert his or her lost, separate identity.

> *Anthony Storr*   24.1.8

It is ridiculous to think you can spend your entire life with just one person. Three is about the right number. Yes, I imagine three husbands would do it.

Clare Booth Luce 19.7.81

I recommend to everybody who has been through a tough time – go back to your original husband.

Sarah Miles 16.6.85

Maybe a younger man appreciates me. The older ones are impotent and young girls don't know the difference.

Zsa Zsa Gabor on her planned eighth marriage 3.8.86

When a man opens the car door for his wife, it's either a new car or a new wife.

Prince Philip 6.3.88

A woman should have a trim waist, a good 'up top' and enough down the bottom, but not too big!

Duchess of York 27.7.86

I don't ask my husbands for anything. I give them presents when I leave them and never ask for alimony.

Zsa Zsa Gabor, on her sixth marriage 11.10.81

I've tried to be factual and as unemotional as possible.

Sara Keays 10.11.85

I think it's inevitable that in this country there will be a woman president.

Ronald Reagan 27.11.88

A good marriage is at least 80 per cent good luck in finding the right person at the right time. The rest is trust.

Nanette Newman 11.10.81

I never put on an ounce – it doesn't matter what I eat.

Princess of Wales 8.6.86

Some of us have become the men we wanted to marry.

> *Gloria Steinem, founding editor of Ms magazine, New York*
> 4.11.82

Women do not want to turn back the clock, but they fear the world.

> *Anne Summers, Ms editor*   3.1.88

Life is so unfair. You're probably 80 before you know the ground rules for understanding between the sexes.

> *Anna Ford*   31.3.85

There is only one political career for which women are perfectly suitable: diplomacy.

> *Clare Booth Luce*   11.10.81

One wants to mutter deeply that apart from having two good legs I also have two good degrees and it is just possible that I do know what I'm talking about.

> *Edwina Currie*   7.11.86

I've never said to myself I'll never marry again.

> *Elizabeth Taylor*   22.6.86

I don't think a prostitute is more moral than a wife, but they are doing the same thing.

> *Prince Phillip*   11.12.88

If you want to know about a man, you can find out an awful lot by looking at who he married.

> *Kirk Douglas*   11.9.88

If somebody fancies another bloke's girl, he's got to ask him if he has finished with her.

> *Jimmy Savile*   17.4.83

Being a sex symbol has to do with an attitude, not looks. Most men think it's looks, most women know otherwise.

> *Kathleen Turner, actress*   27.4.86

Adultery in your heart is committed not only when you look with excessive sexual desire at a woman who is not your wife, but also if you look in the same manner at your wife.

Pope John Paul II 12.10.80

It's a well-known saying that the women lost us the Empire. It's true.

Sir David Lean 24.2.85

Women are not going to understand what is happening in Afghanistan or what is happening in human rights.

Donald Regan, White House Chief of Staff 24.11.85

My mother was always the boss in the house.

Edda Mussolini Ciano 21.11.82

I don't want to die. Ought I to feel guilty about that?

Commissioner Catherine Bramwell-Booth, on her approaching 100th birthday. 29.5.83

You don't know a woman until you've met her in court.

Norman Mailer 5.6.83

I shrug my shoulders in despair at women who moan at the lack of opportunities and then take two weeks off as a result of falling out with their boyfriends.

Sophie Mirman, Businesswoman of the Year 3.4.88

Women are getting stronger. But we're still in a transitional state, rather like the trade unions.

Elizabeth Jane Howard 11.7.82

The Labour Party is being led by a woman, but she has not been elected to anything. She is the lady who makes the breakfast in the Kinnock household. That is who is leading the Labour Party, and she is leading it by the nose.

Edwina Currie 22.2.87

You have to admit that most women who have done something with their lives have been disliked by almost everyone.

> *Françoise Gilot, artist and former mistress of Picasso* 11.10.87

You know, you can only perceive real beauty in a person as they get older.

> *Anouk Aimee* 28.8.88

Do not give me any tosh about open marriages – that's just another way of saying fast and loose.

> *Anna Raeburn* 19.6.83

There are some who think First Ladies should be kept in attics, only to say lines, pour the tea and then be put away again.

> *Nancy Reagan* 10.5.87

If your home burns down, rescue the dogs. At least they'll be faithful to you.

> *Lee Marvin* 28.9.80

Being married six times shows a degree of optimism over wisdom, but I am incorrigibly optimistic.

> *Norman Mailer* 17.1.88

I don't think men and women were meant to live together. They are totally different animals.

> *Diana Dors* 8.5.88

I believe in marriage, old-fashioned marriage.

> *Joan Collins* 14.12.86

Don't talk about marriage – it brings me out in a rash.

> *Joan Collins* 26.4.87

Women expect to be loyal to the first man they love.

> *Gong Yijuan, agony aunt, Peking Evening News* 3.4.83

Women have gradually lost confidence in themselves and in their ability to give birth.

> *Dr Wendy Savage* 7.9.86

You can run the office without a boss, but you can't run an office without the secretaries.

> *Jane Fonda* 1.2.81

It's very dangerous if you keep love letters from someone who is not now your husband.

> *Ms Diana Dors* 14.9.80

I've had that feeling of falling in love quite a few times. It's rather like being put under anaesthetic.

> *Diana Dors* 29.6.80

I married a doctor. I was going to marry the barmaid but she was on duty that night.

> *Richard Gordon* 21.6.81

If women had been consulted more often, we should not be in half such a mess as we are today.

> *Baroness Llewelyn-Davies* 20.6.80

Hair, in fact, is probably the bane of most women's lives.

> *Ms Joan Collins* 21.9.80

Eighty three per cent of the money is spent by women. They understand they can't spend more than the old man brings home.

> *Senator Barry Goldwater* 14.12.80

My mother said it was simple to keep a man, you must be a maid in the living room, a cook in the kitchen and a whore in the bedroom. I said I'd hire the other two and take care of the bedroom bit.

> *Jerry Hall* 6.10.85

There is a widely-held view, even among pro-monarchists, that nobody does more damage to the institution of monarchy than this wayward woman.

> *William Hamilton MP on Princess Margaret* 6.4.80

Women who work are much more likely to wander than those who don't.

> *Piers Paul Read*   24.7.83

It is ironic that the wife who made Britain great again, and who is the leader of the Western World, has to get her husband to sign her tax form.

> *Jacqui Lait at the Tory conference*   11.10.87

Some women would feel they would be fulfilling a more important role if they were carrying weapons.

> *Mr Francis Pym, Defence Secretary*   6.4.80

Women have smaller brains than men.

> *Hojatolislam Rafsanjani, Speaker of the Iranian parliament*   20.7.86

If women got a slap round the face more often, they'd be a bit more reasonable.

> *Charlotte Rampling*   6.3.83

I don't bring my work into the bedroom. Once we are in bed we talk about Dickens.

> *Edwina Currie*   29.3.87

I don't know any uneducated women.

> *Lady Antonia Fraser*   22.9.85

The Prime Minister likes to be flirted with, but Michael doesn't find her at all attractive.

> *Anne Heseltine*   19.1.86

It is concerning that an MP and a Minister could suggest that you actually have to be a Member of Parliament in order to have an opinion or to campaign for issues that concern you.

> *Glenys Kinnock*   22.2.87

If women are treated as second-class citizens, they will behave like them.

> *Dr Shirley Summerskill, MP.*   20.1.80

How do you sit in a restaurant with a man who earns about a sixth of what you do and expect him to pay?

Sue Barker   15.6.80

I really wish my bust was smaller.

Samantha Fox   2.2.86

Good looks are almost a stigma. You have to try harder to prove you're intelligent.

Debra Sue Maffett, retiring Miss America   25.9.83

I've never yet met a man who could look after me.

Joan Collins   26.7.87

It contains a misleading impression, not a lie. It was being economical with the truth.

> *Sir Robert Armstrong, on one of his letters*   23.11.86

I will never get married again.

> *Elizabeth Taylor*   28.2.82

His talk made you feel you were living in heaven.

> *Enid Bagnold on Frank Harris*   22.6.80

It is more than a coincidence that the majority of traitors in this country since the war have been loners, perverts or drunkards.

> *Sir Bernard Braine, MP.*   14.11.82

Though the English pride themselves on their sense of humour, they distrust humorous men.

> *Lord Annan*   2.11.80

This is a deeply moral society.

> *Rupert Murdoch*   31.7.88

I'll cut everybody's hands off.

> *Ayatollah Khomeini*   14.6.81

Every Cork man is shy until his second pint. After that, you can't shut him up.

> *Professor Brendan Kennelly*   20.11.88

I'm not a dictator. It's just that I have a grumpy face.

> *General Pinochet of Chile*   11.5.86

We will see, once again, coalition government in this country.

> *Dr David Owen*   4.1.87

There is a place in society for awkward questions.

> *Jonathan Aitken, MP.*   8.2.87

In any riot situation head injuries are a risk.

> *Dr John Burton, Hammersmith coroner*   1.6.80

I find all this money a considerable burden.

> *John Paul Getty II*   15.12.85

To ask the Queen for a cigarette is rock bottom.

> *Jeffrey Bernard*   18.7.82

I need a drink!

> *Denis Thatcher in the week of his son's wedding*   15.2.87

After we deal our reprisal blow we'll call it quits.

> *Mir-Hossein Moussavi, Iranian Premier*   25.10.87

What I'd like to do is to die on stage in the middle of a good performance and with a full house.

> *Sir John Gielgud*   25.3.84

Never let the other fellow set the agenda.

> *James Baker, US Secretary of State*   20.11.88

I will exterminate the filthy little worm.

> *The Marchioness of Reading, on Mr Dai Llewellyn* 16.3.80

I would die for my country but I could never let my country die for me.

> *Neil Kinnock* 5.10.86

One is always on the run, looking for a place to hide.

> *Edna O'Brien* 19.10.86

That supervisor was the biggest cow I've ever met in my life.

> *Joan Collins at Heathrow* 29.3.87

My brother will be remembered as a great art historian.

> *Wilfred Blunt* 3.4.83

In the end it comes back to love. Marie's last words to me were words of love.

> *Gordon Wilson, Enniskillen bomb survivor* 3.1.88

We think we have reached the bottom of the pit of degradation when a still deeper level of man's inhumanity is dug.

> *Bishop Cahal Daly* 31.10.82

I'm just a crazy bastard who wanted to climb the towers of power.

> *Marcus Morgan after his discovery on the roof of 10 Downing Street* 22.12.85

If you're accused of something long enough, you do it in the end.

> *Fiona Richmond* 4.11.82

I'm a great believer in the good sense of the British people and the great tides of history.

> *James Callaghan* 12.4.87

I sensed I was being drawn into an authorised, but deniable, operation.

> *Peter Wright* 30.11.86

I regret that I haven't made any money.

> *Sir Robin Day*   8.5.88

Graveyards have a morbid reputation. Many people associate them with death.

> *The Bishop of Bath and Wells*   17.4.88

Water is a burning issue.

> *Ieuan Owen, Plaid Cymru candidate at Gower*   5.9.82

Will the Government take steps to have the horse recognised as an agricultural animal?

> *Harry Greenway*   12.6.81

All I ever wanted was a nice little house in North Oxford and a don for a husband.

> *Lady Wilson*   24.2.80

The 50 or so invitations you receive a week are sent not because those people are dying to see you but because of the position you hold. If you don't believe me, ask one of your predecessors how fast they stop.

> *Donald Rumsfeld, advising White House staff*   18.12.88

The biggest misconception about me is that I am a very negative person, anti-social and uneducated.

> *Sylvester Stallone*   19.6.88

I'm just not in a position to comment.

> *Phyllis Oakley, State Department, on reports that George Shultz has a tiger tattooed on his left buttock*   25.1.87

I've never had a gold Rolls-Royce.

> *Sir David Napley*   15.1.84

People look at me and automatically assume I'm a yob. And that bothers me because I'm not.

> *Bob Geldof*   4.5.86

A substantial number of people of working age appear to have withdrawn, temporarily or permanently, from the labour force.

> *Bank of England Quarterly Bulletin* 28.12.80

I think it's 60 per cent likely that Western civilisation will destroy itself in 20 or 30 years' time.

> *E. P. Thompson* 20.12.81

I have no doubt that the elderly are going to die this winter. Surgeons are going to die. We are all going to die eventually.

> *Edwina Currie* 2.7.87

I'm trusting in the Lord and a good lawyer.

> *Lt-Col Oliver North* 7.11.86

The spoken word is like a sped arrow that cannot be recalled.

> *Roy Mason* 8.12.85

Personally I hope never to see any ice ever again.

> *Sir Ranulph Fiennes* 8.8.82

You snivelling little git.

> *Brian Sedgemore, MP, to Nigel Lawson* 22.12.85

If your name is on the bullet, there is nothing you can do about it.

> *Prince Charles* 26.4.81

I believe that the result of the Battle of Hastings dealt a blow to brevity from which our language has never recovered.

> *Lord Kings Norton* 1.2.81

Believe it or not, we are just as fed up with the weather as everyone else.

> *Spokesman for the London Weather Centre* 13.7.80

I have not made a study of the question but believe that it is a minor point in the history of war.

> *Jean-Marie Le Pen on the Holocaust* 20.9.87

Weddings always end with people tearing each other's hair out.

Barbara Cartland   12.7.82

About one tiger in 12 has an untrustworthy character.

John Aspinall   5.10.80

There are only two sorts of people in life you can trust – good Christians and good Communists.

Joe Slovo, ANC chief   6.11.88

We were expecting some old jalopy from Djibouti to turn up, but it was magic seeing the Britannia, like a fairy story.

Lucian Lemanski. Aden evacuee   26.1.86

I know a little more this time.

Eddy Shah   28.8.88

I didn't take an antagonistic attitude towards her at all.

Edward Heath on the Prime Minister   30.10.88

I'm the last Charleston dancer.

Lord Grade   24.4.88

I have loved justice and hated iniquity: therefore I die in exile.

Peter Wright, quoting Pope Gregory VII   14.12.86

Throwing stones certainly teaches people a lesson.

Ayatollah Khalkhali   13.7.80

I do have a heart.

Henry Kissinger   28.2.82

A weed is simply a plant that you don't want.

John Simmons, curator of Kew Gardens   17.7.83

I don't know that I'm in the twentieth century. I may be in the eighteenth or twenty-first.

Mr Ian MacGregor   18.1.81

He has a nasty instinct for the exposed groin, and always puts his knee in just to stir things up.

> *Austin Mitchell on Norman Tebbit*   5.2.89

If there is some task I can do in the interests of the country, I would do it.

> *Mr Edward Heath*   22.5.88

I'm not particularly interested in being Prime Minister. It's a lousy job. I don't want it, and there are others who can do it.

> *Norman Tebbit*   11.10.87

If God gives me life beyond 1990, when I shall be 67, then I shall be concentrating on my golf.

> *President Zia of Pakistan*   14.12.86

I find inspiration in my studies of animal behaviour.

> *Ken Livingstone, leader of the Greater London Council*
> 12.7.81

I survived the Russians and the Gestapo, so I am ready to do battle with the Inland Revenue.

> *Lord Kagan*   15.6.80

The answer to darkness is to turn on the light.

> *Lord Hailsham*   12.7.81

I am not interested in a third party. I do not believe it has any future.

> *Shirley Williams*   25.5.80

No one says anything bad about a turtle.

> *Patricia Riexinger, Office of Endangered Species, US Fish and Wildlife Service*   19.7.81

I'm pretty fed up with being known as Nancy Mitford's brother-in-law.

> *Duke of Devonshire*   1.6.80

A woman rang to say she'd heard there was a hurricane on the way. Well, don't worry. There isn't.

Michael Fish, BBC Weatherman 18.10.87

You have a right to speak, and a right to be wrong. And you exercise both rights extensively.

Neil Kinnock to Ken Livingstone 29.11.87

On my tombstone I want the words, 'I made it work.'

Elizabeth Esteve – Coll, new Director of the Victoria & Albert museum 10.1.88

Fighting makes you forget your tiredness and makes you active.

Ayatollah Khomeini 9.1.83

No dog is worth risking a life for.

Daily Mirror 9.1.83

I'm going towards 40. I've spent long enough using easy charm to get by.

Nigel Havers 15.1.89

You never forget people who were kind to you when you were young.

Mark Birley 29.1.89